ENTERTAINING MATHEMATICAL TEASERS

and How to Solve Them

ENTERTAINING MATHEMATICAL TEASERS

and How to Solve Them

J.A.H. Hunter

Dover Publications, Inc., New York

Published in Canada by General Publishing Company, Ltd., 30 Lesmill Road, Don Mills, Toronto, Ontario.
Published in the United Kingdom by Constable and Company, Ltd.

Entertaining Mathematical Teasers and How to Solve Them is a new work, consisting of problems (some corrected and amended) selected from the author's syndicated column, "Fun with Figures," and first published in book form by Dover Publications, Inc., in 1983.

Manufactured in the United States of America
Dover Publications, Inc., 180 Varick Street, New York, N.Y. 10014

Library of Congress Cataloging in Publication Data

Hunter, J. A. H. (James Alston Hope)
  Entertaining mathematical teasers and how to solve them.

  1. Mathematical recreations.   I. Title.
QA95.H778   1983   793.7'4   82-18298
ISBN 0-486-24500-4

PREFACE

All too many people leave school hating math! But don't blame the subject—a distaste for math is often the fault of dreary and unimaginative teachers. Math can be fun, and this new selection of rather easy teasers stresses the fun side of the subject.

Yet again my thanks are due to the thousands of loyal newspaper readers without whose ideas and continued support this little book would never have been published.

Have fun!

Toronto, 1983   J. A. H. HUNTER

CONTENTS

TEASERS

TEASERS

1 THE LUMBERJACK

Said a feller out felling a tree,
"My age I've divided by three.
The result is a square,
Yet my age, I declare,
Is six times a cube. Glory be!"

2 A MATTER OF IDENTIFICATION

"I've only met one of them," said Martha. "The guy with the beard. Which is he?"

"You figure it out yourself," Clem replied. "Two of them are married, two have blue eyes, and two are clean-shaven. The bearded one has brown eyes. Doug's wife is Ken's sister, and the bachelor has the same color eyes as Joe. They're three great guys."

Who had the beard?

3 A CHANGE OF PLAN

Doug was putting up a fence at the end of the lawn. "You planned to have the posts five feet apart, so you told me," said Linda, coming out to watch. "But you've got them more than that."

"I didn't think you'd notice," Doug chuckled. "But I found I was four posts short, so they had to be seven feet apart to do the same job."

How long was his fence to be?

4   THE MAILING

Lucy looked at the boxes on her desk. "We've got plenty of these leaflets," she said. "Four thousand were printed. Do you remember how many we had last year?"

"Not exactly, but we didn't mail that many," Joe replied. "I did notice there was always one over when I divided the number by any number from two through nine."

How many was that?

5   AGES

"So you've got five kids, with the one girl in the middle," said Alan. "How old is she?"

Clem smiled. "Figure it out yourself," he replied. "They're all spaced two years apart, and the youngest boy is just half as old as the oldest."

How old was the girl?

6   SIMPLE DIVISION

Peter glanced at the boy's figuring. "Just a regular four-digit number," he said. "What's so very special about it?"

"Look, Dad," Stan replied. "To divide it by seven you only have to drop its second digit."

He was right, so what was the number?

7   A DEAL IN STAMPS

"I bought three lots of stamps today," Joe told his wife. "Nearly a hundred in all."

"And I try to save pennies!" Ann sighed. "Anything good?"

Joe nodded. "Maybe. They averaged 66¢ in one lot, $1.68 in the second, $3.08 in the third. It's funny that I paid exactly the same for each lot."

How much was that?

8   NOT HIS FAULT

Joan was waiting there right under the clock. "You're five minutes late," she said. "What happened?"

"Traffic, Mom," Jeff replied. "Not like most days at this time. I was driving at a nice steady speed to get here ten minutes early. But the last ten miles I could keep to only half that speed."

What was his speed for the first part of the run?

9   THE SHARING

Uncle Fred emptied the little envelope onto the table. "Some stamps I saved for you two kids. Just sixty-five in all."

The children started picking. "Thanks a lot," said Susan. "Half each?"

"Not exactly," Uncle Fred replied. "You're the older, so share them in the ratio of a half to you and a third to Jack."

How would that work out?

10   SOCIAL WORKERS

"I haven't seen you for quite a while," said Eve. "Are you still a volunteer at that Youth Center?"

Susan shook her head. "No, it was open only a few weeks, twenty-eight days to be exact. And not very strenuous," she replied. "There were three of us on duty every day, and each of us put in only six days."

How many volunteers did that entail?

11   A NEW OUTFIT

"Wow!" exclaimed Sally, when her husband came in. "New shoes, new tie, new shirt. Don't say they came free."

Mike grinned. "Only ninety-nine bucks the lot," he told her. "The shoes cost three times as much as the tie and shirt together, and the shirt cost a quarter as much as shoes and tie together."

What did he pay for the shoes?

12   NO GUESSING HERE

When Ken was half as old as Kate,
His cousin Jean was thirty-eight.
When Kate was half as old as Jean,
Then Ken himself was seventeen.
Their ages total one one three,
So what must those three ages be?

13   TRUST DAD

Bert handed the boy some money. "There you are, the change from your ten dollars," he said. "You'd better check it."

"Thanks, Dad. I know it will be okay," replied Joe. "But did you notice something? When you multiply the cents by the dollars you get one more than half the total amount in cents."

How much was it?

14   KIDS LIKE APPLES

"Bill was right. I did buy too many apples for the kids' party," Celia declared. "I got two for each child invited."

Maggie smiled. "That sounds reasonable."

"Yes, but a quarter of the kids didn't show up," Celia replied. "Sixteen boys came, and the surplus provided just one extra apple for each girl."

How many apples had she bought?

15   THE FAMILY

Amelia looked at the old photo. "It wasn't such a big family for those days," she said. "I had twice as many brothers as sisters."

Andy nodded. "That sounds a lot."

The old lady smiled. "Well, my brother Albert had as many sisters as brothers."

You figure it out!

16   DOWN TO THE FARM

"What stock have you got?" John asked. "Only hogs and geese?"

Jake nodded. "That's right, it's only a small farm," he replied. "Just forty heads and eighty-eight feet."

How many hogs did he have?

17   TOO COLD FOR COMFORT

"Do you remember that cold spell last year, our first real snow for years?" Tony asked. "You wanted me to drive into town."

"You wouldn't, so we missed a good party," Karen replied. "I'm not likely to forget. But what was the actual temperature?"

Her husband thought a moment. "A rather interesting one," he told her. "The Fahrenheit and the Celsius readings both had 5 as their last figure."

What were those readings?

18   COMPLETE CONFUSION

"Steak or chops? I just don't know," said Linda. "What's the price of that steak?"

Sam smiled. "Well, it will cost you one dollar less than a chop and a half would cost if two and a half such chops cost you two dollars less than three of the same steaks."

What a way to treat a lady! Maybe you can figure it out.

19   POKER CHIPS

Jack dipped into the little cloth bag, and pulled out a red poker chip. "The odds against a red were just five to two," Mike told him. "They would have been two to one against you getting a green chip."

"Okay," said Jack. "I know you have only the three colors in there, so what were the odds against my drawing a blue?"

What do you think?

20   A MATTER OF CHANGE

"That was fun, but it cost you a lot," said Ann as they left the restaurant. "You didn't seem to get much change from the cashier."

Ken smiled. "It was okay," he told her. "If the check had been half what it was I would have got three times as much change, but if it had been two bucks more my change would have been half what it was."

How much was the change?

21   FIGURES DON'T LIE

Bill was teasing his teenage sister. "You're only a kid," he told her. "When you're as old as I was when you were a third as old as I am, I'll be twice as old as you are now."

He was quite right, so how old was the girl?

22   MAYBE LATER

Steve looked up at the big clock and then checked his watch. "Say, that's funny," he told his wife. "The hour hand is right on a minute mark and the minute hand is exactly one minute behind it."

"Okay, dear." Ann smiled. "But it's too early in the morning for teasers."

What was the time?

23   A WORK OF ART

Joe was examining his friend's treasures. "A nice piece," he said, picking up a richly enameled rectangular box. "From China, eh? What's its volume?"

Bob smiled. "I got it in Canton on a business trip to Shameen many years ago," he replied. "You figure out its volume. The bottom is ninety-six square inches, the side seventy-two, and the end forty-eight square inches."

Well?

24 QUITE A DEAL

A cunning old codger called Kaid
Got eighty-four bucks for some jade.
His profit per cent,
In cents for the gent,
Was half the amount he had paid.

How much was that?

25 BEFORE INFLATION

It was in the good old days, and Steve had been standing quite a while watching the kids as they came in for pop and candy. "They all want those nuts at six cents an ounce," he commented. "You must have sold near ten pounds of them while I've been here."

"Not that much," Charlie replied. "But it's sure funny the way they've gone. Dollar for pound, and cent for ounce, I've taken exactly the same amount for them as the total weight I've sold."

How much was that?

26 FOR WINTER PLANTING

"What's this?" asked Elsie, opening the paper bag. "Bulbs for the spring?"

Les smiled. "Just a few tulips and daffodils for the house," he replied. "It's funny. For each sort I got ten fewer than the price per bulb in cents, but the tulips came to $7.99 more than the daffs."

How many of each had he bought?

27 INFLATION

"I'm broke," said Ted. "The previous Christmas I averaged nine dollars on little gifts for the few who got them. But this Christmas I spent thirty bucks more on gifts for the same people."

"So what?" Fred chuckled. "You've only got nieces and nephews to think about."

Ted smiled. "Them and one sister too," he replied. "The previous Christmas I spent exactly as much on the nephews as on the nieces, and the same total on my sister. This time her gift cost me seven dollars more, and I spent five dollars more on each nephew and four dollars on each niece."

How much had he spent on those gifts this time?

28 WHAT'S OLD?

Dave shook his head. "Sure, I like her," he said. "But she's quite old, Dad."

"That makes me senile!" Mike chuckled. "Now you just figure out how old Aunt Susan is. Her age is three times what you get when you add its digits together."

How old was that?

29 ALL VERY NEIGHBORLY

Bob took back the photo. "It was a long time ago," he said. "They both married, but we keep in touch. Kate has a nice home at Glynn, and Jane lives at Brent."

"Quite close, eh?" Andy commented. "How far is Brent from here?"

"Well, I'll put it this way, as you used to like teasers," Bob replied. "Via Glynn it's seventeen miles further than if you drive there directly. To Glynn via Brent is nineteen miles more than the direct route, and from Brent to Glynn via here is thirteen miles more than it is direct."

How far, then?

30 CHECK AND MATE

Steve was at home when the boys came in. "How did you make out in the chess tournament?" he asked them.

"Pretty good, Dad," Bill replied. "We played the same number of games. Ron won two-thirds of his and I lost only one of mine."

"That's right," Ron agreed. "We had no draws, so between the two of us we won three-quarters of our games."

They obviously made a good team. How many games did each boy play?

31 CARS THAT PASS ON THE WAY

It was Sam on the phone. "I passed you on the road today. Didn't you see me?" he asked. "I left Torbal at exactly noon and arrived in Brent just thirty-six minutes after we passed. My usual steady speed all the way, of course."

"That's odd. I did see you, but too late. And I left Brent at noon and got to Torbal forty-nine minutes after we passed," Tony replied. "I did my usual fifty-four miles per hour all the way."

What was Sam's speed?

32 DADDY KNOWS BEST

"It's only teenage infatuation," Tom declared. "I do like Bob, but he's double your age."

"Come on, Dad, that's nothing these days," Cathy replied. "He doesn't look it, and anyway three years ago the digits of my age added up to the same as the digits of his age did."

What they call a *non sequitur!* But how old was she?

33 TWO BIRDS INSTEAD OF ONE

Fred came in with a shopping bag. "They didn't have a large capon," he said. "So I got two birds instead, exactly nine pounds the two."

"That's fine," Ann told him. "What did you pay."

"$5.28 for the bigger one, $3.64 for the other," Fred replied. "The small bird was 8¢ a pound more."

What were the respective weights?

34 WHODUNIT

The four kids were there by the broken glass when Ron ran out. "Who did it?" he cried.

"Not me," John told him. "It was Pete."

"It wasn't Pete at all," said Sam. "John did it."

Peter grinned. "Well, it wasn't me, and Ann didn't do it either," he declared.

Ann just said nothing.

In fact each boy made one true statement and one false. One of the four was guilty, but which one?

35 HARDWARE

Tom was in his little store when I dropped in for a visit. "That's a real bargain at $43.89," I commented, noting the sturdy construction and fine finish of an electric scroll saw standing on the counter. "Not much profit for you at that price."

"Enough for me, and I'll make a sale." The old man chuckled. "But here's something for you. My markup on it is exactly the same percentage as what I paid for it in dollars."

Neat! But what had it cost him?

36 BOYS AND GIRLS

There was an old lady in Sheen,
Whose grandchildren numbered sixteen.
Four-ninths of the boys
Were too old to want toys,
So how many girls must that mean?

37 JACK AND JILL

When Jack was twice as old as Jill was when Jack was twice as old as Jill was when Jack was half as old as he is now, Jill was half as old as Jack was when Jill was a year older than half as old as Jack is.

Both are in their twenties, and we have of course taken ages in completed full years.

How old are they?

38 THINGS HAVE CHANGED

"Don's doing fine," said Ken. "He gets only $1.60 an hour less than I do."

Old Jake shook his head. "$1.60! That's more than I made in a day when I started!" he exclaimed. "You must be making a bit yourself now."

"Not bad," Ken replied. "It takes me only seven hours to earn what Don earns in nine."

What was Ken's hourly rate?

39 A DEAL IN ONIONS

"You're selling these onions in pairs," said Amanda. "What if I only want seven?"

"No problem. They're all the same, so take your pick and I'll be glad to split a pair," Hank replied. "Two dollars for seven for you, lady, and it gives me only the same profit as I make on one pair."

Amanda smiled. "That's quite a deal, but I'll take a dozen."

The old man thought a moment. "That's near twice as many," he told her. "I'll want just double the profit for that lot, so they'll be $3.50."

What was his regular price for a pair of onions?

40 ONE BIGGER, ONE SMALLER

"You know what you told me about our car's license-plate number, Dad," said Alan. "I've found two other numbers that work that way."

"So we're not unique." Harry smiled. "A regular six-figure number. You just shift the right-hand pair of digits to the left-hand position in front of the other four in order to multiply the number by three."

"That's it," the boy agreed. "But there are three of them, one bigger than ours and one smaller."

What was their number?

41 THE CRUTCH

"How can I remember this number?" Sarah asked. "I need one of your gimmicks."

Stan glanced at her book, and thought a moment. "You shouldn't need one for only two different digits," he told her. "But you do get it if you add the square of its first digit to twice its last."

What was the page number?

42   THE LUCK OF THE DRAW

Paul had cards on the table when Ken came in. "A quiz for you, Dad," he said. "Look."

Ken smiled. "Two piles of cards," he commented. "Do you have a complete deck there?"

"Sure, but no jokers," the boy replied. "It's two to one against red if you draw one card from the bigger pile. But, if I shift a black from that to the small pile it will be three to one against drawing a black from the smaller pile."

How many blacks and reds were in the larger pile?

43   A DOUBLE BIRTHDAY

"Your birthday today and also your son's!" Andy exclaimed. "That's amazing. How old is he now?"

Bob smiled. "I'll tell you with fractions," he replied. "One over his age, plus one over my age, makes one over seven. That's one-seventh, of course."

So what were their respective ages?

44   NO WATCH

It was hot and humid in the office that afternoon. Gwen looked over to where Sam was checking his books. "What's the time?" she asked.

The old man smiled. "No watch again, eh?" he replied. "Well, it's just twice as many minutes before five as it's minutes since three o'clock."

What was the time?

45   A MATTER OF AGES

Susan put down her pencil. "Grandpa is just twice as old as you are, isn't he, Dad?" she asked.

Tom nodded. "That's right, but why?"

"Well, it's funny about your ages," the girl replied. "If you add four to the first figure of your age and take away four from the last figure you get his age."

Susan was right, so how old was Tom?

46 NO CREAM?

"My coffee's getting cold," said Keith. "I'm waiting for cream and sugar."

The girl didn't seem too concerned. "Sorry, sir," she replied. "I'll fetch you some, but most folks here don't use them."

Keith shook his head. "Is that so? Well, I've been checking your other customers," he told her. "Twelve have taken sugar, seven have taken cream, three have taken both, and only two have taken neither."

How many other customers were there?

47 A HAND FOR DAD

Bill seized the handles of the lawn mower. "You've done enough, Dad," he said. "Let me finish."

"Okay, I've mowed all around for a width of five feet," Tom replied. "That leaves just the square inside for you to do, so I figure you'll do four square feet less than I've done."

What were the dimensions of the lawn?

48 THE HAREM BEAUTY

There was a fair maid in Rabat,
Who was plump, not excessively fat.
The square of her weight,
When divided by eight,
All in pounds was a cube. How was that?

49 GOSSIP

The little old ladies were having a fine old gossip, but now they had nearly come to blows over two young men of their acquaintance.

"Bill married Judy, and Doug married Ann," Miss Prim declared.

Of course Mrs. Pothersniff had to disagree. "Bill married Eve, and Doug married Judy," she insisted.

In fact, neither of them was wholly wrong. So who married whom?

50 JUST A BALL

For quite a while John had been fingering the children's gaily colored ball. "I guess it's only a coincidence," he said, "but there's something rather special about this."

"Just a regular play ball," Mary replied. "We've seen lots of them. What's the gimmick?"

"Its size," John replied. "Its volume in cubic centimeters comes to seven times its area in square centimeters."

What was its diameter?

51 NEW BROADLOOM

Bill put down the newspaper. "It says $9.50 a yard," he said. "How is that measured, Dad?"

"They mean area," Tom replied. "Square yards."

"That's easy, then. I was trying to figure out what wall-to-wall would cost for my square room," the boy explained. "That way I'd require five yards more than the total measurement around the edge."

How big was his room?

52 THE TEST

Bertie put down the sheet of paper. "Fifteen questions in all, with some toughies," he commented. "How did you both make out?"

"Clare answered twice as many as I missed," Kim replied. "And she missed exactly a third as many as I answered."

How many had each of them answered?

53 A SPECIAL OCCASION

"It's okay with your buddies, but you don't take me to places like that," said Ann. "What did it cost you?"

Mike chuckled. "Come on, you know it was our annual reunion," he replied. "The dinner came to only $99.97 for the lot, so we were able to split it equally among all of us."

What had it cost him then?

54 JUST PHONE NUMBERS

"That's funny," said Karen, putting down her pen. "If you divide any of those three phone numbers by ours you always get exactly the same remainder."

Ron looked up. "That's quite a coincidence, but what phone numbers?"

"Ted's, Aunt Mary's and Uncle Alan's," the girl replied. "2153, 4387 and 7738."

What was their own number?

55 FREUD HAD A WORD FOR IT

"How old's your Dad?" Karen asked. "He looks much older than mine."

"That's ridiculous," Betty told her angrily. "But you can figure out his age if you like. It's three times its first figure, added to five times its last."

How old was that?

56 THE CHECK

"I'll pay a quarter of the check, and also a quarter," said Sam. "That's more than my share, but I'm rich."

"You're lucky. I'm near broke," Andy commented. "I can pay a quarter of the balance, and also a quarter."

"That's okay with me," declared Bert, picking up the check. "I've got ninety-eight cents and that just covers the rest."

What was the total?

57 STILL COVERED

Terry looked down over his son's shoulder. "Hi, that's my fire-insurance policy!" he exclaimed. "Don't tell me it's lapsed."

"Nothing like that, Dad. Just something interesting I found about its number," the boy replied. "It's the smallest that has its cube root and also its seventh root different whole numbers."

What was the number?

58 BIG BROTHER TALKS

Mike grinned. "I'm as old as the total of what you and Pete were three years ago."

"So what?" Joe replied. "Pete's twice as old as I was three years ago, and I'm half as old as you'll be in three years' time."

What were their ages?

59 WHEN FRIENDS MOVE

"I hope I've got their new addresses right," said Clare, putting down her pen. "Greg at number 45 and Jerry at 53."

"You should know!" Roy chuckled. "But I'd say 45 is Jerry's number and Greg's is 35."

In fact, each of them had one number right and one wrong.

What were the respective numbers?

60 THAT LADY OF LEE

There was a young lady of Lee,
Whose age had its last digit three.
If you total the two,
Which is easy to do,
One less than a square you will see.

61 QUITE A COINCIDENCE

Jill emptied her purse onto the table. "That's all I've got, just three pennies," she declared. "Look."

"Okay, you made your point." Ted smiled. "But that's funny. They all turned up heads."

What are the odds against that happening?

62 THE MATH CLUB

"How goes the math club?" Bob asked. "You told me you started with under a dozen the first week."

"That's right, Dad," Jack replied. "The following week we got three new members, and each week since then there have been two more new members than we got the week before."

Bob was surprised. "That's great, but how many have dropped out?"

The boy smiled. "None," he declared, "and now we've got fifty-four members."

How many did they start with?

63   THIS OR THAT

Betty liked them both. "Which one shall we have?" she asked her husband. "This rug is six inches shorter but four inches wider than the other."

"I don't know, dear," George replied. "The man said they're both exactly twelve square feet, and they both look good to me. Let's toss for it."

What were the dimensions of the shorter rug?

64   HIGH FINANCE

"We checked our money yesterday. Remember?" said Brenda. "I had just three-quarters as much as you, but now you've got one dollar more than me."

Susan nodded. "That's right, and now you have just two-thirds what I have, so you've spent twice as much as I have."

How much did Susan have left?

65   TIME FLIES

Mike had found the drive into town from the airport most interesting. "So many changes since last time," he said. "And now I guess your kids are pretty well grown up. They were all teenagers when I was here."

"You've got a good memory." Doug chuckled. "It's odd that their three ages multiplied together come to 6336 and that's my license-plate number!"

What were those ages?

66   WHEN DAD GOES SHOPPING

"They didn't have a turkey, so I got these two chickens instead," said John. "This one's just a pound heavier than the other."

Martha looked. "That's fine. What did you pay?"

"$2.17 for the small one and $2.61 for the big one," her husband replied. "The big one was 4¢ a pound cheaper than the other."

What were the prices per pound?

67   THE NEW PRINCIPAL

"How do you like the new job?" asked Elsie. "It must be quite a change after a big city school."

"It sure is, only 348 pupils in all," John replied. "There are 231 below Grade 5, but 165 above Grade 3."

How many in Grade 4?

68   NONE FOR MOM

"None left!" exclaimed Linda. "How many did you buy?"

"I'm not sure, Mom, but we didn't think you'd want any," Brian replied. "Les took a third of them and one-third of a plum, then Betty took half of what remained and also half a plum, and that left only five for me."

How many had they bought?

69   NOT ODD? THAT'S ODD

Ron put down his pen. "You know our number is three times the number of Aunt Enid's home?" he asked his father.

Charlie thought a moment. "That's right, I never noticed before. But what of it?"

"Well, I just found something else. Our two numbers together use all five even digits, zero through eight, once each."

What were the two numbers?

70 WHO'D THINK OF THAT?

Sam looked up when Martha switched off the TV. "That's better," he told her. "Now I can think."

"Okay." His wife smiled. "So what's the big thought?"

"Only the ages of Jim and Jane," Sam replied. "Her present age is a third of what his will be in twelve years' time, and seven years from now her age will be just double what his was seven years ago."

You figure it out.

71 BURRA-BURRA

"It's good of you," Linda declared. "But what's that funny-looking fish you're holding up?"

Clem glanced at the photo. "That? The natives call it burra-burra, but it was new to me," he replied. "Its head was half as long as its body, the tail was a third again as long as the head, and the body was three inches shorter than head and tail together."

How long was it?

72 STRANGE BUT TRUE

The square of nine is 121!
It looks a trifle queer,
But still I say it's really true
The way we figure here.

And nine times ten is 132:
The selfsame rule, you see.
So what d'you say I have to write
For five times twenty-three?

73 THE GAMBLERS

Bob gathered up the cards. "I'm through," he said. "If I lost another dollar I'd have lost just two-thirds of what I started with."

"Okay, but you could win it all back," Jim told him. "A while ago you said you'd lost half your money."

"No dice!" Bob laughed. "I've lost five bucks more since then."

How much did he start with?

74 A SHOPPING SPREE

"That's all I've got left," said Clare, taking a dollar from her purse. "Money goes so fast."

"Well, you were in three different stores," Harry replied. "Do you know what you spent?"

His wife smiled. "Sure, I do," she told him. "In each store I spent exactly two-thirds of what I had in my purse, plus two-thirds of a cent."

How much had she spent in all?

75 UP AND DOWN

"These ties don't seem to be selling as they used to," said Charlie. "They were always popular."

"They were, indeed," his wife told him. "But then you upped the price 25%. Remember?"

Charlie nodded. "Okay. Let's reduce it 25% and see what happens. That will be $3.75."

What had been the original price?

76 THERE AND BACK

"Thirty-one miles each way, and mostly hills. That's quite a ride," said Joe. "How long did it take you?"

Peter smiled. "Twice as long coming back as I took to get there, not counting stops," he replied. "And hills! Only one mile of level road each way. I averaged eighteen miles an hour downhill, fifteen on the level, but only five miles an hour uphill."

What was his actual riding time coming back?

77 LUNCHEON FOR THREE

"How about that!" Bert exclaimed. "I forgot my wallet, so I can only pay ninety-seven cents."

Dick glanced at the check and passed it to Ron.

"We all had the same, but it's okay," he said, putting some money down on the table. "Here's fifty cents more than my proper share, and Ron can take care of the rest."

Ron chuckled. "You'd be in real trouble without me, but anyway here's the balance. It's half as much again as you've paid, Dick."

What was the amount of that check?

78   THE WISE GUY

"What about the stamps I sent for you and Judy?" Tom asked. "Were they any good?"

Kim smiled. "Sure. They were great. Judy got three more than half what she would have had if I'd kept three more than half what she got."

"Okay, okay." Tom shook his head. "How many did you keep?"

"Just two more than I gave her," the boy replied.

How many stamps had Tom sent?

79   AT THE MEAT MARKET

"That's right, lady. Only eighty-eight cents a pound," said Sam, taking the bird off the scales. "This one weighs three-fifths of its weight, plus three-fifths of a pound."

What was the price?

80   AGES AND AGES

Three years ago Ann was half again as old as Roy was when Ann was a year younger than Roy is now.

When Roy is five years older than Ann will be when Roy is as old as Ann is now, Ann will be twice as old as Roy is now.

What are their respective ages?

81 BOYS WILL BE BOYS

Doug was yawning when he came down for breakfast. "What time did you come home last night?" Amy asked. "I didn't hear you."

"Not so late, Mom," the boy replied. "I checked with your clock, and the minute hand was exactly on a minute mark seventeen minutes ahead of the hour hand."

What time was it?

82 HER SECRET

"My age?" answered Barbara Blatt.
"Just keep it right under your hat.
Adding one to each figure
Makes it nineteen years bigger
Than half what it is." So what's that?

83 ONLY CANS

"I ordered those cans," said Bill, handing his partner an invoice. "There's the bill, and you'll notice they didn't add any tax."

Ben checked the amount. "Just the two prices," he commented. "But it's funny about the total. The cents are the number you got at thirty-nine cents, and the dollars are the number at forty-nine cents each."

How many had been bought at each price?

84 UNEQUAL SHARES

"Good news today," Doug told his wife. "They've cleared up Aunt Amelia's estate, making exactly $14,934 to be shared by us four nephews."

"Great!" Mary exlaimed. "That's more than three thousand dollars each."

Doug smiled. "Not really. The old dear stipulated

that the division should be in the proportions of one-third to one-quarter to one-fifth to one-sixth. I get least as I'm the youngest."

How much would he get?

85 THE DRIVE

Harry stopped the car at the main entrance. "Here we are, exactly seven minutes late," he said. "This time I kept to a steady thirty miles per hour just to please you."

"I know, dear, and a few minutes doesn't really matter," Amelia told him. "Last time we did the trip you were five minutes early, and we started the same time as today."

"That's right." Harry nodded. "But we had kept to a steady thirty-six miles per hour."

How far had they come?

86 GIVE AND TAKE

"I'll give you one-third of what I have," said Stan, checking his money on the table. "Don't forget it next time I'm broke."

Martha shook her head. "I don't need it all," she told him. "But you do that, and I'll give you back a quarter of what I have now."

They did what she suggested, and so ended up with $1.45 each! How much did Stan start with?

87 BIG BROTHER

"You're just kids," declared Doug. "I'm as old as your two ages added together."

That was too much for Karen. "Okay," she replied. "But you're only a teenager anyway, and our two ages make three times your age if you multiply them together."

How old was Doug?

88 ALIENS AT HOME

Glumph watched as his wife fed the wrygans. "They look half starved," he commented. "But they were a real bargain for twelve trigos."

Lozla shook her head. "Come on," she replied. "At Xuppys they're one trigo less a dozen, so you'd have got two more for the money."

How many had Glumph bought?

89 A LUCKY BREAK

"That was terrific, winning $402 at bingo," said Ken. "I guess you gave your kids a treat to celebrate."

"Nothing much." Greg smiled. "I spent a dollar each on a fancy gift card for each of them. Then I split the balance into as many equal parts as I have children, and divided up one part equally among them in one-dollar bills."

"Very nice, too," his colleague commented. "I've met three of your kids, but how many do you have?"

You figure it out.

90 TIES FOR DAD

Fred took out his wallet. "This morning you told me you had exactly ten dollars," he said.

"I know, but I got you those three ties since then, and that's left me only $1.60," Karen replied. "The green cost a third again as much as the blue, and the blue cost one-third as much as the other two together."

What were the prices?

91 A PARADOX

"Ages are funny," said Mike. "As Betty gets older I seem to get younger."

Tom smiled. "That's ridiculous," he told the boy. "How come?"

"Well, look," Mike replied. "Two years ago I was

three times her age, but in two years time I'll be only twice as old."

It did sound a bit odd! How old was Mike?

92 THE MOVE

"We've lived here a long time, Dad," said Susie. "When did we move from Tulla Trail?"

Stan smiled. "Just sixteen years ago," he replied. "I was six times as old as you were, but now you're a big girl and half my age."

How old was Susie when they moved?

93 ALL THE WAY FROM CHINA

Sam placed the packet with the others. "That's enough for now," he said. "Folks don't appreciate fine tea like they did."

"You can say that again, but what's the blend you've been making up?" asked Fred. "I see you'll sell it at $4.48 a pound."

"That's right, a mixture of pure oolong and lapsang souchong," the old man replied. "I pay $3.29 a pound for the oolong and $2.38 for the lapsang, and my markup is only 60%."

What were the proportions in his blend?

94 JUST IF

If my 4 were a 9,
And my 6 were a 3,
What I am would be one
Less than half what I'd be.

I'm three little digits,
Just three in a row,
So what in the world
Can I be? Do you know?

95 HE BROKE THE BANK

Bobbie was smiling happily as he checked his cash on the table. "All that from your piggy bank?" Gwen asked. "How much in all?"

"About three bucks, Mom," the boy replied. "I just figured that if I had half as many dollars in bills, and twice as many cents in coins, there would be just three cents more."

How much did he have there?

96 TAKE A CARD

"It's a complete deck, no jokers," said Mike, putting the cards down on the table. "Take as many as you like but leave me some."

Clive did just that. "What now?" he asked. "If you drew a card from what I have the odds against it being black would be exactly three to one."

Mike handed him four blacks from the cards that remained on the table. "Okay, I'll tell you the game in a moment," he replied. "But if you drew a card from what's on the table now, the odds would be just three to one against it being red."

How many cards had Clive taken?

97 IT'S RELATIVE

"Your new math teacher sounds nice," said Doug. "Is she young?"

Sheila shook her head. "Not really, Dad," she replied. "She told us her age is just three times the product of its digits."

How old would that be?

98 FRESH FRUIT

John lowered the big bag onto the kitchen table with a sigh of relief. "I got enough fruit to last us a week," he told his wife. "Thirty-seven in all of the sorts you wanted."

"Fine," replied Cathy. "Then you didn't forget mangoes."

"I like them too," her husband declared. "I got some melons and five times as many pears, and four times as many oranges as I got mangoes."

How many of each?

99 SOUVENIRS

Harry and John wanted to see more, but their wives insisted on taking a break for coffee at the little restaurant.

Sitting there, the four compared the souvenir cards they had purchased while wandering through the zoo. It turned out that each couple had bought a dozen. Harry had three more than Susan, and Jane bought only two.

How many cards did John buy?

100 THE NUMBER MAN

"What was their number?" Amelia asked. "I bet you made up something on it."

"Doris and Ken?" Stan thought a moment. "Sure, I did," he replied. "If you subtract its two figures separately from five times what you get by reversing their order you'll get it."

You don't have to guess! What was the number?

101 NOT HER PROBLEM

Judy was waiting when the two boys came back with the candies they'd bought. "Let me have some," she said. "I'll pay my share."

"Okay, we'll divide them equally between us but it will cost you forty cents," Bob told her. "Ron got forty-five cents' worth, and I paid seventy-five cents. They're all the same, so let's figure out how he and I should split your money."

What do you say?

102 NOT REALLY OLD

Martin shook his head. "Nancy is younger than that," he declared. "Just three years ago she was a quarter as old as I was."

"That could make her quite ancient!" Jane chuckled. "I still don't know your age."

"A big secret," Martin told her. "But in three years' time I'll be three times as old as Nancy will be."

What were their ages?

103 ON THE ROAD

Greg drew level again with his friend as they cycled along the quiet road at a steady twelve miles per hour. "That was another blue bus, like the one that overtook us exactly twenty minutes ago," he shouted.

"Yes, the next one on the same run," replied Joe, checking his watch. "And right on schedule. There's one every fourteen minutes this time of day."

What was the average speed of the buses?

104 THIS OR THAT?

"I'll have the print anyway," said Greg. "And one of these two frames. What's the difference?"

Sam checked his list. "With the gilt frame the total is $87.75," he replied. "But the black frame is only two-thirds the price of the gilt, so with that it would come to an even $75.00."

What was the price of the print alone?

105 IN THE MIRROR

Harry looked up at the wall. "It can't be that late!" he exclaimed. "The clock's crazy."

"Seems okay to me," Ted told him. "What's wrong?"

"The time, of course," Harry replied. "It says twelve minutes after seven."

His friend was smiling. "You need glasses! You're looking at its reflection in that big mirror on the opposite wall."

No peeking at a watch, now! What time did the clock show?

106 LEAVE OF ABSENCE

"Exactly two hundred," you say?
But it's seven whole months to the day.
You're fifteen days short
In your adding, old sport,
For those seven months I'm away.

What months would he be away?

107 THE TESTS

"We had to answer all the questions, just 'Yes' or 'No,'" Fran explained. "The first paper I got only five wrong."

Ben smiled. "That sounds good. What about the other paper?"

"Tough, but the same number of questions," the girl replied. "I got just a third of them wrong, so over all I got 75% right for the two papers."

How many questions in each paper?

108 THEY'RE NOT THAT CHEAP NOW!

Betty bit into one of the candies. "They're good," she said. "How many did you get?"

"Figure it out if you want to know," her husband replied. "I'd have got eight more for the dollar I paid if they had been a nickel a dozen less."

How many?

109   FIGURES, FIGURES

"Figures can be so interesting," said John. "But you wouldn't see it the way I do."

Peter smiled. "It depends on the figures," he declared. "But you don't mean what I'd mean."

"Maybe not, but take my age," John told him. "If you add it to its two digits you get the same digits in reverse order."

How old was he?

110   DOLLARS AND CENTS

"What was that price?" Elsie asked. "I thought I'd remember."

Andy smiled. "Not me, I used a gimmick," he told her. "It was four times its cents, added to three times its dollars. You figure that one out."

You try.

111   A BUILDING LOT

"So you've bought a bit of land, eh?" said Frank. "Tell me about it."

Jeff smiled. "It's nothing special, Dad," he replied. "A rectangle just 9,009 square feet, and fine for a small house."

"Sounds good!" Frank commented. "What frontage?"

"I forget exactly, but it's forty feet less than the depth."

You figure it out.

112   IN THE BAG

"Is that all you got?" Jane asked, watching as her husband emptied his fishing basket onto a dish.

"It was one of those bad days for me, but we caught about two dozen between the three of us," Joe replied. "I got half as many as Mike, and Mike caught one more than a quarter of what Steve and I got together."

How many had Joe caught?

113 FAIR'S FAIR

Eddie examined the set of three identical stamps. "I'd like one," he said. "But that's all, and anyway I've only got $56.00 on me."

"Okay. Here's $70.00 to make up the $126.00 for the lot," Joe told him, taking the money from his wallet. "I'll keep one, and we'll surely sell the other to someone."

So the two friends left the store with their purchase. And that same day they sold the third stamp to another man at a profit: he paid them $60.00.

Then came the problem! How would they share the $60.00 fairly?

114 NO SECRET

Florence shook her head. "You can figure it out yourself," she told the boy. "If you add the two digits of my age together and subtract that from my age you get my age reversed."

"Reversed?" Bobby asked. "You mean same digits but in the opposite order?"

"Sure," the lady replied.

How old was she?

115 THE WINNER

Jeff was excited. "Look what I got, Mom," he cried. "A first prize in the slogan competition. Two bucks."

"That's great," Joan told him. "How many prizes were there?"

"Twelve in all," the boy replied. "Second prizes were one dollar each, and there were consolation prizes at seventy-five cents. That's thirteen dollars in prizes."

How many second prizes?

116 AT THE LUNCH COUNTER

Harry picked up the check. "Okay, we did agree to split it evenly between the three of us," he said. "What I had came to only $2.43, so be my guests."

"Not me," Greg told him. "Jim certainly saves 82¢ that way, but I'll be paying 45¢ more than the price of what I had. Anyway, I'm happy."

What was the total amount?

117 AT THE CLUB

"I had lunch at the Club," said Sandy. "Just four of us, but you'd never believe the names of the other three guys."

Lucy smiled. "Try me. I always say they're a bunch of weirdos there anyway."

"Okay. Their names were Law, Tooth and Painter. And they work in the three corresponding professions, although none in the one indicated by his name," Sandy replied. "Mr. Tooth is married to the lawyer's sister, so can you figure out the dentist's name?"

118 A LITTLE OLD LADY

"You want my age?" said Auntie Liz.
"You shouldn't ask, but here it is.
You switch its digits: that will show
Just half my age ten years ago."
The clues are there, so you can see
How old dear Auntie Liz would be.

119 IT'S A FAKE

"That's really something!" Andy exclaimed. "A 1912 silver dollar. Do you have any more?"

John smiled. "I've got eight of them, but one's a good fake. It looks exactly the same but it's a bit heavier."

Andy thought a moment. "Okay, then tell me how you would identify it for sure with only two weighings if you had a balance scale but no weights."

That was too much for John, but you figure it out.

120 PROGRESS

Sam paused in the doorway. "Well!" he exclaimed. "What a change from last time I was here. You must have at least thirty clerks now."

"No, not that many yet." Mike grinned. "If we had twice as many girls or three times as many men, then we'd have thirty. But wait another year or two."

How many clerks?

121 WIN OR LOSE

Susan watched the two men finish a game. "No more tonight," she told them. "Coffee's ready and you've neglected me all evening. Who won?"

"We both did," Peter replied. "Jack didn't win in half the games we played, and I didn't win in two-thirds of them. Two games were drawn."

How many had Peter won?

122 A RURAL SCENE

Ron got back into the car. "Did you see those cows when you honked?" he asked. "It was like a signal for them."

"Not especially, but they're all still there, around twenty in all, I guess," John replied. "What d'you mean?"

The boy smiled. "A fifth of those standing lay down, and a quarter of those lying down stood up, so then half of them were down and half were up."

How many in all?

123 MALE CHAUVINISTS

"Four girls to every three boys?" Greg commented. "That sounds like a good party!"

Jerry grinned. "It was, Dad," he replied. "But if there had been seven more boys it would have been the other way around."

How many girls were there?

124 SUBSCRIPTIONS

Jack emptied his wallet. "That's all I have, just fourteen bucks," he said. "Anyway it will help."

"That's great," Martha told him, noting the amount on her list. "So far I had collected an average of $2.22 per head, but now you've hiked the average to $2.41. Thank you so much."

How much was her new total amount?

125 A NEW NUMBER

"What's your new number?" Karen asked. "I know it's the same exchange."

Fred nodded. "Maybe this will help you remember," he replied. "The middle two digits are the same, and if you multiply them together you get the last digit. All four digits add up to twenty-three."

What was that number?

126 WHO WANTS A SQUARE?

Keith was looking out the window. "You've changed your patio," he said. "It used to be square."

"That's right, but Susan thought that's become a dirty word." Clem chuckled. "So we made it four feet longer and took three feet off the width, and now it's only one square foot bigger than it was."

What were the new dimensions?

127 IT MAKES SENSE

If nine times ten
    were one three two—
That's just the way
    it's read—
Then what d'you think
    you'd have to say,
For nine times
    five instead?

128 THEY MET AGAIN

"That's right. Ted and our two girls," said Jim. "They're evenly spaced with Ted in the middle."

Charlie smiled. "It's years since I saw them," he declared. "How old are they now?"

"Figure it out," Jim replied. "The square of Ted's age is twice the difference between the squares of the girls' ages, but six years ago it would have been half again as much instead of twice."

What were the three ages?

129 A MATTER OF FOURS

"Loan me four bucks," said Donna. "I'll pay you back tomorrow."

Mac checked his cash. "I don't have that much," he told her. "But here's something funny. If I had four dollars more and four cents less I'd have just three times what I've got."

That didn't help his sister, but how much did he have?

130 WHAT? US?

Tony smiled. "I guess it is funny about their ages," he said. "But what about ours?"

"Us!" Jill exclaimed. "What d'you mean?"

"Just think," Tony replied. "My first digit is twice the second digit of your age, and my second is twice the first digit of your age, yet I'm only six years older than you."

What were their ages?

131 THE HANDICAP

"I'll race you to the corner," said Bill.

"Okay," replied Betty, stopping beside him on the sidewalk. "But give me a bit of a start."

She ran ten steps forward and then stopped. "That's fair because you run five steps while I run six, but four of your steps are as long as five of mine."

Bill gave the signal and the race began. But they reached the corner together, showing that Betty had been right.

How many steps did Bill run?

132 THE MORNING AFTER

"What a stench!" exclaimed Mary, opening the window. "You must have smoked that whole box of fifty El Stumpos."

Kim chuckled, picking a cigar from the box. "Not that many," he told her. "Twice the number we smoked is just three more than half what remain in the box right now."

How many did remain?

133 SHARE AND SHARE ALIKE

"Let me have some," said Betty when the two boys showed her the candies they had bought. "I'll pay."

"Fine," replied Ken. "They're all the same. I paid sixty cents, but Steve only had forty-five cents so he paid that. You give us thirty-five cents and we'll share them all evenly."

His brother nodded. "That's okay with me. But how do we divide her thirty-five cents?"

What would you say?

134 LONG, LONG AGO

"It was during the First World War," said Celia. "Don't you remember?"

Jim chuckled. "Sure, I do, and I remember something else about that day," he told her. "Dad re-marked that there were exactly six times as many days after it in the month as there were days before it."

What was that date?

135   FOR A GOOD CAUSE

"Some people are mean," declared John. "We collected only $50.84 for the Firemen's Fund."

Lucy nodded. "That's not mean."

John smiled. "Listen. There are eighty-eight of us in all," he replied. "It was a dollar each for men but only half of us gave. The women were nearly as bad. Only two-thirds of them donated, averaging just ninety-four cents each."

How many men contributed?

136   MERCHANDISING

"You know those crazy mod belts we bought," said Dan. "Last night I noticed we'd sold only twenty-six of them, so I cut the price from $6.95 to $4.99."

Carol nodded. "A good idea, but that's a heck of a discount."

"Sure, but it's paid off already today," her husband declared. "At the new price we've sold fifty-five, and our profit on them is $6.75 more than it had been on the others."

The belts were all the same, so what had Dan paid for them?

137   JUST FIGURES

My two little digits, you see,
Make a perfect cube added to three.
But if added, it's seen
That they total thirteen.
So what in the world can I be?

138 SORT THAT ONE OUT

When Mike was twice as old as Judy was when Mike was three times as old as Judy was when Mike was as old as Judy is now, Judy was half as old as Mike was when Judy was half as old as Mike is now.

We have taken ages in complete years, so how old are these two?

139 THE GIRLS NEXT DOOR

Joe was at the window. "There go the three Lang girls," he said. "A funny lot, they all look the same to me. Always in red or blue."

"Eve, Ann and Carol. Nice kids, but they do have a thing about those two colors," Cathy told him. "Ann wears blue if and only if Eve is in red, and you never see Carol and Ann both in blue. That's Carol or Eve in the red mini, but they wouldn't both be wearing red."

What color was Ann wearing?

140 THE BIRD LOVER

It was quiet in the pet shop, quiet except for the happy chatter of the birds. "What happened to your finches?" Mary asked. "You had a lot last week."

Cecil smiled. "I've still got eleven," he replied. "Only two sales since you were here. An old lady bought a third of what I had, plus a third of a finch. And then a couple of kids took a third of what was left, plus a third of a finch."

How many had the old lady bought?

141 A BAD YEAR

"How was your peach crop?" Andy asked. "We figured last year that you'd averaged exactly as many per tree as the number of trees you had."

"That's right, but this year the average was only ninety-seven per tree," Stan replied. "That's thirty-five hundred down on last year's total for the same number of trees."
How many trees?

142 FRACTIONS

"Let's have some!" The kids crowded around Betty as she checked the candies. "Okay, but I'll have a few myself," she told them. "It's by age. A third of them for Bill, a quarter for Eve, a fifth for Linda, and a sixth for Bruce. That leaves just six for me."
How many were there in all?
NOTE: Based on a problem written 1,400 years ago by the great Indian mathematician Brahmagupta.

143 WAITING

"He'll be here at seven o'clock," said Doreen. "Only a few more hours to wait, but what's the time now?"
Tom glanced at his watch. "It's the third time you've asked, so figure it out yourself now," he told her. "Add a quarter of the time till seven o'clock this evening to a fifth of the time since noon, and that'll be the time."
What was it, then?

144 VACATION TIME

"So the boys went off on their own," said Jill. "Did they go together?"
"Not this year," replied Alan. "One went to Tulla for the fishing, one went to Skerrig, and one to Brent. Don hates fishing."
Jill smiled. "Me too, but they say it's relaxing."
"Sure," Alan agreed. "Anyway, Don wouldn't go to Brent, and Harry has a thing against Tulla."
Where did each of the three go?

145   NO CHILDREN

"That was quick," said Susan, helping her brother out of his coat. "Were there many at the meeting?"

Doug smiled. "Only thirty-seven in all, and no kids. All people we know," he replied. "There were four other single men, and all the marrieds were with their spouses. I counted twenty women."

How many married men?

146   THE OLD HOME

"They don't put in solid oak beams any more," said Steve. "How old is the house?"

Gary smiled. "Dad says it was fifteen years old when he was born," he replied. "And here's something odd. The square of its age has my age as its second half, and Dad's age as its first half."

How old was the house?

147   MENTAL ARITHMETIC

Peter put down his pen. "We were talking about gimmicks for quick multiplication," he said. "Look at this."

Mike looked. "Okay. That's a four-figure number and you've put a 3 at the end and a 3 in front. So what?"

"Well, that multiplied it by forty-three," Peter replied. "Isn't that something?"

What was the original four-digit number?

148   SHE FORGOT

"What was that number?" Donna asked her husband. "I forgot to write it down?"

"Okay. Then figure it out yourself," Stan replied.

"It's nineteen more than one perfect square but eighteen less than another perfect square."
What was that number?

149 THREE IN A ROW

If my first were a 4,
And my second a 3,
What I am would be double
The number you'd see.

For I'm only three digits,
Just three in a row.
So what must I be?
Don't say you don't know!

150 RIDING SCHOOL

"So you fell off today!" Steve chuckled. "You have to do that before you can ever hope to be a good rider. Were there many in the class?"
"Just us and the staff, and of course the horses. Forty more feet in all than heads," John replied. "There were thirteen more heads than tails."
How many horses?

151 MORE TRAINS

"More trains!" Joan exclaimed. "And I bet they cost plenty. Couldn't you have done with one book?"
"No, and anyway they were both bargains," her husband replied, picking up one of the massive volumes. "If this had been double its price they would have cost twenty-eight dollars together, but if the other had been double, the two would have been thirty-two dollars."
He's a railroad buff, but you can figure out the prices of those books.

152 1066 AND ALL THAT

"I've been reading about William the Conqueror and his invasion of England," said Steve. "Most interesting."

Sam smiled. "What a battle! But they were tough."

"Sure, even the kids," Steve declared. "There was one young boy who became a big shot later. The book says he died on an anniversary of the battle, and when his age was one-seventeenth of the year he was born."

What year did he die, then?

153 A MATTER OF TIME

Harry had been gazing out of the window for quite a while, watching the children at play in the sunshine. "Is it eleven yet?" he asked. "My watch is on the blink."

"Past that," Don replied. "In fact it's exactly six times as many minutes after the half hour as the hour hand is minutes before twelve o'clock."

What was the time?

154 THE RENDEZVOUS

Don was there already when Judy arrived. "What kept you?" he asked. "I started right away after your call. Didn't you?"

Judy smiled. "Sure, and I averaged forty-two miles an hour all the way. You must have speeded."

"Not really, but I did have three miles more to do than you," Don replied. "So I averaged fifty-six miles per hour, and that got me here twenty minutes before you."

How far did he have to drive?

155 WOT? NO CRYSTAL?

Charlie put down the bottle. "New glasses, eh?" he said. "And fancy ones at that. I bet they cost plenty."

"Less than twenty bucks the lot, and the small ones

cost me fifty cents more than the others," Ann replied. "If you really want to know, the larger glasses were ninety-seven cents each, the small fifty-nine cents."

How many of each had she bought?

156 AT THE PUMPS

Charlie was checking. "I see you sold seventy-four spark plugs today," he said. "That's great, but how come so many?"

"Just regular service. Eight-cylinder, six-cylinder and four-cylinder cars," replied Ben. "A full set for every car, and there were twice as many fours as sixes."

How many eight-cylinder cars?

157 THE REC ROOM

"When d'you plan to finish the rec room?" Alan asked. "It looks like a rectangular barn right now with no furniture and the floor not done."

Greg smiled. "It's the vinyl tiles. I'm trying to decide between nine-inch squares at nineteen cents and twelve-inch at twenty-nine cents each," he replied. "No wastage with either and Gwen prefers the smaller tiles, but they'd cost us $33.11 more for the complete floor."

What were the dimensions of the room?

158 NEARLY BROKE

"Let's have two dollars," Jill begged. "I'll pay it back Friday for sure."

Jack emptied his pocket. "I don't have that much. There's all I've got, just pennies and dimes. If the dimes were nickels and the pennies quarters, I'd have one dollar more than I've got."

How much did he have?

159 THE QUESTION

Aunt Amelia had been a good teacher in the days of the little red schoolhouse, and she still remembered.

"That's a big secret, but you can figure it out if you really want to know," she told Tony in reply to his question. "If you switch the two figures of my age, reverse their order, you'll get a third of what my age was five years ago."

You try!

160 THE TRAIN BUFFS

Mike had made the trip many times. "That's the morning express from Tulla we're passing," he said. "It left Tulla one hour after we pulled out from Brent, but we're just 25% faster."

"That's right, and we're also passing Cove, two-thirds the distance between Brent and Tulla," Martin agreed. "So we're both right on schedule."

Obviously a couple of train buffs! Assuming constant speeds and no stops, how long would it be before they reached Tulla?

SOLUTIONS TO TEASERS

SOLUTIONS TO TEASERS

1 THE LUMBERJACK

Say age $6X^3 = 3Y^2$, where obviously X is less than 3. Then $Y^2 = 2X^3$, and "at sight" $X = 2$. Age 48 years.

2 A MATTER OF IDENTIFICATION

The men are Joe, Doug and Ken, and Doug is married. The bachelor is not Joe, so Ken is the bachelor and he has the same color eyes as Joe. Hence Ken and Joe have blue eyes. Then Doug has brown eyes and is bearded.

3 A CHANGE OF PLAN

Say $(X + 1)$ poles 7 feet apart, total distance $7X$ feet. Doug had intended $(X + 5)$ poles 5 feet apart, for distance $5(X + 4)$ feet. So, $7X = 5X + 20$, hence $X = 10$. The length of the fence was to be 70 feet.

4 THE MAILING

Say $(n + 1)$ leaflets. Then n is divisible without remainder by all numbers from 2 through 9. The minimal such number is $(9 \times 8 \times 7 \times 5)$, i.e., 2520. But the number mailed was less than 4000, so it was 2521.

5 AGES

Say ages $(x - 4)$, $(x - 2)$, x, $(x + 2)$, $(x + 4)$ years. Then, $2(x - 4) = x + 4$, whence $x = 12$. So the ages were 8, 10, 12, 14 and 16 years, the girl being aged 12 years.

6 SIMPLE DIVISION

Say the number had its first two digits $(x)(y)$ in that order, the final pair of digits being (z). Then, "dropping the second digit," we have $100x + z$. So, $1000x + 100y + z = 7(100x + z)$, whence $150x + 50y = 3z$. But z has 2 digits, so $z = 50$, making $3x + y = 3$, and x is not zero. So $x = 1$, with $y = 0$. The number was 1050.

7 A DEAL IN STAMPS

Say x at 66¢, y at \$1.68, z at \$3.08. Thence, $33x = 84y = 154z$. The LCM of 33, 84 and 154 is $3 \times 4 \times 7 \times 11$, i.e., 924. Say he paid $924k$ cents for each lot, where k is some integer (i.e., whole number). Then $x = 28k$, $y = 11k$, $z = 6k$, making $x + y + z = 45k$. But he bought "nearly 100," so we require $k = 2$. He paid \$36.96 for each lot.

8 NOT HIS FAULT

Say total distance $(y + 10)$ miles. Then $(y + 10)$ miles at $2x$ m.p.h. would have taken $(y + 10)/2x$ hours. In fact y miles at $2x$ m.p.h. took $y/2x$ hours, 10 miles at x m.p.h. took $10/x$ hours. So he took $[(y + 20)/2x - (y + 10)/2x]$ hours longer than expected, hence $10/2x = 15/60$, $2x = 40$. His speed for the first part of the run was 40 m.p.h.

9 THE SHARING

A ratio of "one-half to one-third" is the same as ratio "three-sixths to two-sixths," i.e., 3 to 2. So Jill would receive three-fifths of 65, i.e., 39 stamps, and Jack two-fifths of 65, i.e., 26 stamps.

10 SOCIAL WORKERS

Say X people. The total for the Youth Center was (28×3), i.e., 84 man-days. Each did 6 days "on duty," so $6X = 84$; hence there were 14 volunteers.

11 A NEW OUTFIT

Say shoes $\$x$, shirt $\$y$, tie $\$z$. Then we have the three equations: $x + y + z = 99$, $x - 3y - 3z = 0$, $x - 4y + z = 0$. See Appendix A for procedure, giving shoes $\$74.25$, shirt $\$19.80$, tie $\$4.95$.

12 NO GUESSING HERE

Present ages in years: Kate x, Jean y, Ken $(113 - x - y)$. Say Ken was half as old as Kate was, a years ago. Then $x - a = 2(113 - x - y - a)$, whence $a = (226 - 3x - 2y)$.

At that time Jean was $[y - (226 - 3x - 2y)] = 38$, so we have $x + y = 88$.

Say Kate was half as old as Jean was, b years ago. Then $(y - b) = 2(x - b)$, whence $b = 2x - y$.

At that time Ken was $[(113 - x - y) - (2x - y)] = 17$, hence $x = 32$. But $x + y = 88$, so $y = 56$. The ages were: Jean 56 years, Kate 32, Ken 25.

13 TRUST DAD

Say the amount was $\$x$ and $y\cent$. Then, $xy = (100x + y)/2 + 1$. So $2xy - 100x - y = 2$, whence $(2x - 1)(y - 50) - 50 = 2$, so $(2x - 1)(y - 50) = 52 = 4 \cdot 13$. Tabulate for factors, bearing in mind that $(2x - 1)$ must be odd:

	$2x - 1 =$	1	13
with	$y - 50 =$	52	4
	$x \quad\quad =$	1	7
	$y \quad\quad =$	102	54

But obviously $y < 100$, so the amount was $\$7.54$.

14 KIDS LIKE APPLES

Say $4x$ children were invited. Then, $3x$ arrived, i.e., 16 boys, and say y girls. So, $y = 3x - 16$. But $8x$ apples were bought, so $32 + 3(3x - 16) = 8x$, whence $x = 16$.
Celia bought 128 apples.

15 THE FAMILY

Say x boys, y girls. Then Amelia had $(y - 1)$ sisters, x brothers: Albert had y sisters, $(x - 1)$ brothers.
Hence $x = 2(y - 1)$ and $y = x - 1$, making $x = 4$, $y = 3$. So there were 4 boys and 3 girls in the family.

16 DOWN TO THE FARM

Say x hogs, y geese. Then, $4x + 2y = 88$, and $x + y = 40$. Thence, $x = 4$, $y = 36$. There were 4 hogs, 36 geese.

17 TOO COLD FOR COMFORT

The difference between "boiling point" and "freezing" is $100°$ Celsius or $180°$ Fahrenheit. So every 5 degrees on the Celsius scale corresponds to 9 degrees on the Fahrenheit scale.

Here the temperature was $-5X°$ C, say. That would be $9X°$ below freezing on the Fahrenheit scale. So the temperature was $(32 - 9x)°$ F. That "ended" with 5, so within possible limits of temperatures, $X = 3$ or 13. But from Tony's first statement the temperature could not have been as low as $-65°$ C (i.e., $-85°$ F). Hence we have $X = 3$, making the temperature $-15°$ C or $5°$ F.

18 COMPLETE CONFUSION

Say the price of the steak was $\$X$.

Then, if $2\frac{1}{2}$ chops cost $(3X - 2)$ dollars, $1\frac{1}{2}$ would cost $3(3X - 2)/5$ dollars. So, $X = 3(3X - 2)/5 - 1$, whence $4X = 11$, $X = 2.75$. The price of the steak was $\$2.75$.

19 POKER CHIPS

For odds of "5 to 2 against," the chance of drawing a red must have been "2 in 7," and similarly the chance of drawing a green was "1 in 3." So, for every 21 chips there were 6 reds and 7 greens, entailing 8 blues. Then the chance of drawing a blue was "8 in 21," making the odds "13 to 8" against such an event.

20 A MATTER OF CHANGE

Say the check was for $\$X$, and he paid with an $\$(X + Y)$ bill, receiving $\$Y$ change.

For check $\$X/2$, change would be $\$(X/2 + Y)$, whence $X/2 + Y = 3Y$, so $X - 4Y = 0$.......... (A)

For check $\$(X + 2)$, change would be $\$(Y - 2)$, whence $Y - 2 = Y/2$, so $Y = 4$ .... (B)

Combining (A) and (B), $X = 16$. He received $\$4.00$ change from his $\$20.00$ bill.

21   FIGURES DON'T LIE

Obviously, Bill was older than his sister. So say the ages were: sister x years, Bill $(x + y)$ years. Now work back from the comma:
When sister $(x + y)/3$, Bill $(x + 4y)/3$.
When sister $(x + 4y)/3$, Bill $(x + 7y)/3$.
So, $(x + 7y)/3 = 2x$, whence $5x = 7y$. That entails having x as a multiple of 7, but Bill's sister was in her teens, so $x = 14$, with $y = 10$. Bill was 24 years old, his sister 14.

22   MAYBE LATER

Say the time was X hours and Y minutes. Then, the hour hand would be at the $(5X + Y/12)$ minute mark, the minute hand at the Y minute mark.
So, $5X + Y/12 = Y + 1$, whence $60X - 11Y = 12$. Since X and Y are integers (i.e., whole numbers) that entails having Y a multiple of 12. Say $Y = 12k$, making $5X = 11k + 1$. But $X < 12$, so here we must have $k = 4$, making $X = 9$, $Y = 48$. It was morning, so the time was 9:48 A.M.
NOTE: See Appendix C.

23   A WORK OF ART

Taking dimensions as X by Y by Z inches, we have $XY = 96$, $XZ = 72$, $YZ = 48$. Hence, $Y/Z = 96/72 = 4/3$, so $Z = 3Y/4$. Then $3Y^2/4 = 48$, so $Y = 8$, making $X = 12$ and $Z = 6$. Dimensions 12 by 8 by 6 inches, volume 576 cubic inches.

24   QUITE A DEAL

Say he paid X cents for the jade. Then his profit was $(8400 - X)$ cents. Hence $100(8400 - X)/X = X/2$, so $X^2 + 200X - 1680000 = 0$, whence $X = 1200$. He paid \$12.00 for the jade.
NOTE: See Appendix B.

25   BEFORE INFLATION

Say Charlie sold X pounds and Y ounces at 6¢ per ounce. Then, $6(16X + Y) = 100X + Y$, whence $4X = 5Y$. But $X < 10$, so $X = 5$, $Y = 4$. Charlie had taken $5.04.

26   FOR WINTER PLANTING

Say he bought X tulip bulbs, Y daffodil bulbs. Then $X(X + 10) - Y(Y + 10) = 799$, whence $(X + 5)^2 - (Y + 5)^2 = 799 = 17 \cdot 47$. X and Y are integers, and 47 and 17 are prime numbers, so we may tabulate for factors:

$(X + 5) + (Y + 5) =$	799	47
$(X + 5) - (Y + 5) =$	1	17
$X \quad = $	395	27
$Y \quad = $	394	10

Obviously he had not bought 395 bulbs as "a few for the house." So he bought 27 tulips at 37¢ each, and 10 daffodils at 20¢ each.

NOTE: See Appendix D.

27   INFLATION

Say he had x nephews, y nieces.

This Christmas he spent $(5x + 4y + 7)$ dollars more than the previous Christmas. So, $5x + 4y + 7 = 30$, hence $5x + 4y = 23$, whence $x = 3, y = 2$.

The previous Christmas he spent $54 (i.e., average $9 for 6 people) as follows: sister $18, 3 nephews $18, 2 nieces $18. So "this" Christmas he spent $29 on his sister, $11 each on 3 nephews, $13 each on 2 nieces, a total of $84.

28   WHAT'S OLD?

Say Aunt Susan's age had digits (X), (Y) in that order. Then, $10X + Y = 3X + 3Y$, whence $7X = 2Y$, which entails $X = 2$, $Y = 7$. The lady's age was 27 years.

29 ALL VERY NEIGHBORLY

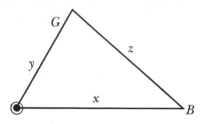

From Bob's statement, referring to the diagram, $y + z = x + 17$, $x + z = y + 19$, and $x + y = z + 13$, so $x - y - z = -17$, $x - y + z = 19$, and $x + y - z = 13$, making $x = 16$, $y = 15$, $z = 18$. Brent was 16 miles from where they were.
NOTE: See Appendix A.

30 CHECK AND MATE

Say Ron played $3X$ games. Then Bill also played $3X$. Ron won $2X$ games, Bill won $(3X - 1)$, so together they won $(5X - 1)$, which was three-quarters of $6X$. Thence $5X - 1 = 18X/4$, so $X = 2$. Each played 6 games.

31 CARS THAT PASS ON THE WAY

Say Sam's speed was X m.p.h., and Brent Y miles from Torbal.
Then, starting at time zero, they passed each other at time $Y/(X + 54)$ hours. Sam reached Brent at Y/X hours, Tony reached Torbal at time $Y/54$ hours.
So, $Y[1/X - 1/(X + 54)] = 36/60$
and $Y[1/54 - 1/(X + 54)] = 49/60$
Dividing, we have: $[X/54(X + 54)] \div [54/X(X + 54)] = 49/36$, whence $X^2/54^2 = 7^2/6^2$, so $X = 63$. Sam's speed was 63 m.p.h.

32 DADDY KNOWS BEST

Say, 3 years "ago" ages were: Bob $(10X + Y)$, Cathy (being in her teens) $(10 + Z)$ years.

"Now," ages would be: Bob $(10X + Y + 3)$, Cathy $(Z + 13)$.

So, $10X + Y + 3 = 2Z + 26$, whence $10X + Y = 2Z + 23$, and also $X + Y = Z + 1$. Combining, $Z = 9X - 22$. But, 3 years "ago" Bob was twice Cathy's age, and $9X$ must be greater than 22, so $X = 3$, with $Z = 5, Y = 3$. The ages were Cathy 18 years, Bob 36.

33 TWO BIRDS INSTEAD OF ONE

Say the larger bird weighed $(9 - X)$ pounds at Y cents a pound, the smaller X pounds at $(Y + 8)$ cents a pound.

Then, $Y(9 - X) = 528$, and $X(Y + 8) = 364$. So, $X = 364/(Y + 8)$ with $(9 - X) = (9Y - 292)/(Y + 8)$. Thence, $9Y^2 - 820Y - 4224 = 0$, giving $Y = 96$ whence $X = 3\frac{1}{2}$. So the weights were $3\frac{1}{2}$ and $5\frac{1}{2}$ pounds.

NOTE: See Appendix B.

34 WHODUNIT

Consider each boy's two statements:

Say John guilty: then John lied twice. John not guilty.

Say Sam guilty: then both Peter's statements were true, so Sam not guilty.

Say Peter guilty: then Sam lied twice. Peter not guilty.

Hence Ann was the culprit.

35 HARDWARE

Say Tom paid $\$x$ for the scroll saw.

Then, $x + x^2/100 = 43.89$, so $x^2 + 100x - 4389 = 0$, making $x = 33$. Tom paid $\$33.00$.

36 BOYS AND GIRLS

The number of boys must be less than 16, but must be divisible by 9. So there were 9 boys and 7 girls.

37 JACK AND JILL

Say ages were Jill x years, Jack $(x + y)$ years, where y could be negative.

Work back from comma:

When Jack was $(x + y)/2$, Jill was $(x - y)/2$.

When Jack was $(x - y)$, Jill was $(x - 2y)$.

When Jack was $(2x - 4y)$, Jill was $(2x - 5y)$.

Now work back from end of paragraph:

When Jill was $[(x + y)/2 + 1]$, Jack was $(x + 3y + 2)/2$.

When Jill was half that, she was $(x + 3y + 2)/4$.

So, $(x + 3y + 2)/4 = (2x - 5y)$, hence $7x - 23y = 2$.

Dividing by 7, we have $(2y + 2)/7$, an integer, so $(y + 1)/7$ is an integer, say k. Then $x = 23k - 3$, and $x + y = 30k - 4$. Both are in their twenties, so $k = 1$, making ages: Jack 26 years, Jill 20.

NOTE: See Appendix C.

38 THINGS HAVE CHANGED

Say hourly rates were: Don x cents, Ken $(x + 160)$ cents. Then $7(x + 160) = 9x$, whence $x = 560$. Ken's rate was $7.20.

39 A DEAL IN ONIONS

Selling price x cents a pair, initial cost y cents each. The profit on one pair was $(x - 2y)$ cents. Then profit on 7 was $(200 - 7y)$ cents.

So, $x - 2y = 200 - 7y$, whence $x + 5y = 200$
. . . . (A)

Profit on a dozen would be $(350 - 12y)$ cents, so $350 - 12y = 2x - 4y$, whence $x + 4y = 175$ . . . . (B)

Combining (A) and (B), we have $x = 75$, $y = 25$.
So Hank's regular price was 75¢ a pair.

40   ONE BIGGER, ONE SMALLER

Say the number was $10000X + Y$, with $X < 100$.
Then $10000X + Y = 3(100Y + X)$, whence $769X = 23Y$. Both 769 and 23 are prime, so say $X = 23\,k$, $Y = 769k$. But Harry described it as a "regular 6-figure number," so Y was a 4-digit number not "starting" with zero. Hence k could be 2, 3 or 4, making the number 153846, or 230769 or 307692. Thence their number was 230769.

41   THE CRUTCH

Say the page number was $(10x + y)$. Then $x^2 + 2y = 10x + y$, whence $y = x(10 - x)$.
But y is a single-digit number, and the two digits were different. Hence $x = 1$, with $y = 9$. The number was 19.

42   THE LUCK OF THE DRAW

Say the larger pile had $2X$ blacks, X reds, the smaller pile $(26 - 2X)$ blacks, $(26 - X)$ reds.
After shifting one black, the smaller pile would have $(27 - 2X)$ blacks and $(26 - X)$ reds. So the odds would be $(27 - 2X)$ to $(26 - X)$ against drawing a black.
Hence, $(26 - X)/(27 - 2X) = 3$, whence $X = 11$.
There were 22 blacks and 11 reds in the larger pile.

43   A DOUBLE BIRTHDAY

Say the ages were: Bob x, son y years.
Then, $1/x + 1/y = 1/7$, so $xy - 7x - 7y = 0$. Hence $(x - 7)(y - 7) = 49$. Obviously $(x - 7) > (y - 7)$, so $x - 7 = 49$, $y - 7 = 1$, making Bob's age 56 years, his son's 8 years.

44 NO WATCH

Say the time was X minutes after 3:00 P.M., so $(120 - X)$ before 5:00 P.M. Then $120 - X = 2X$, so $X = 40$. The time was 3:40 P.M.

45 A MATTER OF AGES

Say Tom's age $(10x + y)$ years, Grandpa's being $(20x + 2y)$ years.

Then, $10(x + 4) + (y - 4) = 20x + 2y$, so $10x + y = 36$.

Tom was 36 years old.

46 NO CREAM?

Say x took sugar, but no cream; y took cream but no sugar; 3 took both; 2 took neither.

Then, $x + 3 = 12$, and $y + 3 = 7$, whence $x = 9$, $y = 4$. Keith's statistics referred to what other customers "have taken," and he had not yet been served. So there were 18 other customers.

47 A HAND FOR DAD

Say the lawn was X feet by X feet. Then Bill would mow a square $(X - 10)$ by $(X - 10)$ feet, and Tom had mown a square of area $[X^2 - (X - 10)^2]$ square feet.

Thence, $X^2 - (X - 10)^2 = (X - 10)^2 + 4$, whence $X^2 - 40X + 204 = 0$, making $X = 34$. The lawn was 34 feet square.

NOTE: See Appendix B.

48 THE HAREM BEAUTY

Say she weighed x pounds. Then, $x^2 = 8y^3$, say, so $x^2 = (2y)^3$. Now, x and y are both integers, so x must be a perfect cube and must be even.

$4^3 = 64$ and $8^3 = 512$, neither being acceptable for the lady's weight. Hence, from $6^3 = 216$, we have her weight as 216 pounds.

49 GOSSIP

If Bill married Judy, then Mrs. Pothersniff would have been wholly wrong. So Bill did not marry Judy.

Then Miss Prim was wrong re Judy, hence she must have been right re Ann and Doug.

So Mrs. Pothersniff was wrong re Doug, whence she must have been right re Bill and Eve.

Doug married Ann, Bill married Eve.

50 JUST A BALL

A sphere or radius R has volume $4\pi R^3/3$, surface area $4\pi R^2$. So here we have (volume) $\div$ (area) = $R/3$ = 7, hence the radius was 21 centimeters and the diameter was 42 centimeters.

51 NEW BROADLOOM

Say room was x yards by x yards.

Then floor area was x^2 square yards, perimeter $4x$ yards. So $x^2 = 4x + 5$, whence $x^2 - 4x - 5 = 0$, making $x = 5$. The room was 15 feet by 15 feet.

52 THE TEST

Say Kim answered X questions, missing $(15 - X)$; and Clare answered Y, missing $(15 - Y)$.

Then, $Y = 30 - 2X$, and $X = 45 - 3Y$, whence $X = 9$, $Y = 12$. Kim answered 9 questions, Clare answered 12.

53 A SPECIAL OCCASION

They "split it equally," so the number at the reunion was a factor of 9997.

$9997 = 769 \times 13$, both factors being prime numbers, so they numbered 13, and each paid $7.69.

54 JUST PHONE NUMBERS

Say $2153 = ax + k$, $4387 = bx + k$, and $7738 = cx + k$, where a, b, c, x and k are all integers (i.e., whole numbers).

Then, $k(b - a) = 2234 = 2 \cdot 1117$, $k(c - b) = 3351 = 3 \cdot 1117$, so $k = 1117$. The phone number was 1117.

55 FREUD HAD A WORD FOR IT

Say his age was $(10X + Y)$. Then, $10X + Y = 3X + 5Y$, whence $7X = 4Y$. Both X and Y are single-digit numbers, so $X = 4$ with $Y = 7$. The age was 47 years.

56 THE CHECK

Say the amount was $4X$ cents.

Then, Sam paid $(X + 25)$ cents, leaving $(3X - 25)$. Andy paid $[(3X - 25)/4 - 25]$, leaving $[3(3X - 25)/4 - 25]$.

So, $3(3X - 25)/4 - 25 = 98$, whence $X = 63$, $4X = 252$. The total was $2.52.

57 STILL COVERED

Say the number was N. Then $N = X^3 = Y^7$, say, where X and Y are integers.

The equation requires $X = k^7$, where k is an integer.

Obviously we cannot have $X = 1$, so the minimal values are obtained with $k = 2$, making $X = 128$, and $N = 2{,}097{,}152$.

58 BIG BROTHER TALKS

Say ages: Joe $(X + 3)$, Pete $(Y + 3)$, Mike $(X + Y)$. Then, $Y + 3 = 2X$, and $X + Y + 3 = 2X + 6$, whence $Y - X = 3$, and $Y - 2X = -3$, so $X = 6$, $Y = 9$.

The ages were: Joe 9 years, Pete 12, Mike 15.

59 WHEN FRIENDS MOVE

Roy gave numbers as: Greg 35, Jerry 45. Clare gave them as: Greg 45, Jerry 53.

Re Roy, if Greg was not at 35, then Jerry was at 45. But, re Clare, in that case Greg would not be at 45, so Jerry would be at 53. Impossible.

Hence Greg was at 35, and Jerry was not at 45. But, re Clare, with Greg not at 45, Jerry must have been at 53.

So Greg was at 35, Jerry at 53.

60 THAT LADY OF LEE

Say her age was $(10x + 3)$. Then, $x + 3 = n^2 - 1$ (say), so $x = n^2 - 4$. Since x is a single-digit number, "at sight" we have $x = 5$. So the lady's age was 53 years.

61 QUITE A COINCIDENCE

1 chance in 2 for the first, 1 chance in 2 for the second, so 1 chance in 4 for both to be heads.

Then 1 chance in 2 for the third, so 1 chance in 8 for all three to be heads.

Hence the odds were 7 to 1 against getting 3 heads.

62   THE MATH CLUB

Say they started with x members. The 2nd week they got 3 new members, the 3rd week 5 new members, so the nth week they got $(2n - 1)$. Hence the total at the end of the nth week was $x + [3 + 5 + \ldots + (2n - 1)]$, which is $x + (n - 1)(2n + 2)/2$, i.e., $(n^2 + x - 1)$.

So $n^2 + x - 1 = 54$, whence $x = 55 - n^2$, which entails $n < 8$. Also, since $x < 12$, we require $n > 6$. Hence $n = 7$, with $x = 6$. They started with 6 members.

63   THIS OR THAT

Say the rugs were X by Y inches, and $(X + 6)$ by $(Y - 4)$ inches. Then, $XY + 6Y - 4X - 24 = XY$, whence $3Y - 2X = 12$. But $XY = 1728$, so $Y = 1728/X$. Substituting for Y, we have $X^2 + 6X - 2592 = 0$, so $X = 48$ with $Y = 36$. The rugs were 48 by 36 inches, and 54 by 32 inches.

64   HIGH FINANCE

Say the previous day Brenda had $3X$ cents, Susan $4X$. Brenda spent $2Y$ cents, Susan spent Y cents.

Susan was left with $(4X - Y)$ cents, Brenda was left with $(3X - 2Y)$ cents. So, $4X - Y = (3X - 2Y) + 100$, and $4X - Y = 3(3X - 2Y)/2$. Thence, $X + Y = 100$, and $X - 4Y = 0$, so $Y = 20$, with $X = 80$.

Hence Susan was left with $3.00.

65   TIME FLIES

$6336 = 9 \cdot 11 \cdot 64 = 18 \cdot 22 \cdot 16$.

When all three were teenagers the ages must have been 13, 15 and 19 years: that being 3 years previously. So the ages were 16, 18 and 22 years.

66 WHEN DAD GOES SHOPPING

Say the larger was X pounds at Y cents a pound, the smaller $(X - 1)$ pounds at $(Y + 4)$ cents a pound.

Then, $XY = 261$ and $(X - 1)(Y + 4) = 217$, so $XY + 4X - Y = 221$. But $XY = 261$ so $Y = 4X + 40$.

Thence, $X(4X + 40) + 4X - (4X + 40) = 221$, so $4X^2 + 40X - 261 = 0$, hence $X = 9/2$, making $Y = 58$. The birds weighed $3\frac{1}{2}$ and $4\frac{1}{2}$ pounds, at 62¢ and 58¢ a pound respectively.

67 THE NEW PRINCIPAL

Say, X pupils in grades below Grade 4, Y in Grade 4, Z in grades above Grade 4.

Then, $X + Y + Z = 348$, $X + Y = 231$, and $Y + Z = 165$. Thence, $X = 183$, $Y = 48$, $Z = 117$. There were 48 in Grade 4.

NOTE: See Appendix A.

68 NONE FOR MOM

Say Brian bought $3X$ plums. Then Les took X and "one third of a plum," so Les left $(6X - 1)/3$ plums. Then Betty took $(6X - 1)/6$ and "half a plum," leaving $(6x - 4)/6$.

So, $(6X - 4)/6 = 5$, whence $3X = 17$. Brian bought 17 plums.

69 NOT ODD? THAT'S ODD

Say the numbers were X and Y, using the digits 0, 2, 4, 6, 8. Then $X = 3Y$ and must have 3 digits.

So the initial digit of X must be the "carry" from 3 times the initial digit of Y. The initial digit of X cannot be zero, so must be 2. To get "carry 2" from 3 times the initial digit of Y, that initial digit must be 8 or 6. $84 \cdot 3 = 252$, $86 \cdot 3 = 258$, neither being acceptable. $64 \cdot 3 = 192$, not acceptable. But $68 \cdot 3 = 204$, so the numbers were 68 and 204.

70 WHO'D THINK OF THAT?

Say the ages were: Jane X years, Jim $(X + Y)$, where Y is a positive or negative integer (i.e., whole number). Then, $X = (X + Y + 12)/3$, whence $X + 2Y = 21$. Thence $X = 9$, $Y = 6$. Jim was 15 years old, Jane 9.

71 BURRA-BURRA

Say the head was $3X$ inches, with body $6X$ inches and tail $4X$ inches. Then $6X = 7X - 3$, so $X = 3$, making the total length 39 inches.

72 STRANGE BUT TRUE

We normally express numbers to base ten. For example, we write the number "four hundred thirty-five" as 435: that is "four times ten squared, plus three times ten, plus five units." In a base-n system, for example, 326 would mean our number $(3n^2 + 2n + 6)$. Words such as ten, forty, hundred are base-ten words and are meaningless when we use some other base: so that base-n number 326 would be read in words as "three two six," not as "three hundred twenty-six."

Say we are dealing with base n here. It will be convenient to carry out our calculations using our normal base-ten system. Then $n^2 + 2n + 1 = 81$ (i.e., the square of nine), whence $n = 8$. So we are working in the base-eight system. That is confirmed by the fact that $(8^2 + 3 \cdot 8 + 2) = 90$ (i.e., nine times ten).

Then, since five times twenty-three is our number one hundred fifteen, we have one hundred fifteen = (one times sixty-four plus six times eight plus three units). That would be read as "one six three" and written as 163 using the base-eight system.

73   THE GAMBLERS

Say Bob had lost $x when he spoke, having started with $y. Then $x + 1 = 2y/3$, and $x - 5 = y/2$, so $x = 23$ and $y = 36$. Bob started with $36.00.

74   A SHOPPING SPREE

Say Clare started with X cents. After the first store she had left $(X - 2)/3$ cents. After the second she had left $[(X - 2)/9 - 2/3]$, i.e., $(X - 8)/9$ cents, after the third $[(X - 8)/27 - 2/3]$, i.e., $(X - 26)/27$ cents. So $(X - 26)/27 = 100$, hence $X = 2726$. She spent $26.26.

75   UP AND DOWN

Say the original price was $100X$ cents. That was increased to $125X$ cents, and then reduced by 25% to $375X/4$ cents. So $375X/4 = 375$, whence $X = 4$. The original price was $4.00.

76   THERE AND BACK

Say on the outward ride it was x miles uphill, y miles downhill. Then his total time going there was $(x/5 + y/18 + 1/15)$ hours, i.e., $(18x + 5y + 6)/90$ hours, and his time returning $(5x + 18y + 6)/90$ hours, so $2(5x + 18y + 6) = 5x + 18y + 6$, whence $8y - 31x = 6$. But $x + y + 1 = 31$, whence $y = 30 - x$. Substituting for y, we have $x = 6$ with $y = 24$. His return ride took 5 hours and 12 minutes.

77   LUNCHEON FOR THREE

Say total $3x$ cents. Then Bert paid 97 cents, Dick $(x + 50)$ cents, Ron $3(x + 50)/2$ cents. The total was $(5x + 444)/2 = 3x$ cents, so $x = 444$. The check was for $13.32.

78   THE WISE GUY

Say Judy received $2X$ stamps, Kim $(2X + 2)$. If Kim had kept $(X + 3)$, Judy would have had $[(4X + 2) - (X + 3)]$, i.e., $(3X - 1)$ stamps. So, $3X - 1 = 4X - 6$, whence $X = 5$. Tom had sent 22 stamps.

79   AT THE MEAT MARKET

Say the weight was X pounds. Then $3X/5 + 3/5 = X$, so $X = 1\frac{1}{2}$. The price, at 88 cents per pound, was \$1.32.

80   AGES AND AGES

Say ages: Roy x years, Ann $(x + y)$ years.
Work back from end of 1st paragraph:
When Ann was $(x - 1)$, Roy was $(x - y - 1)$.
Half again as much as that, is $3(x - y - 1)/2$.
So, $x + y - 3 = 3(x - y - 1)/2$, whence $x - 5y = -3$ . . . . (A)
Work back from end of 2nd paragraph:
When Roy is $(x + y)$, Ann will be $(x + 2y)$.
When Roy is $(x + 2y + 5)$, Ann will be $(x + 3y + 5)$.
So, $(x + 3y + 5) = 2x$, whence $x - 3y = 5$ . . . . (B)
Combining (A) and (B), $x = 17$, $y = 4$. Ages were Roy 17 years, Ann 21.

81   BOYS WILL BE BOYS

Say the time was x hours and y minutes.
Then the hour hand was at the $(60x + y)/12$ minute mark, the minute hand at the y minute mark.
So, $y - (60x + y)/12 = 17$, whence $11y - 60x = 204$. We have x and y as integers, so the general solution for that equation is: $x = 11k + 1$, $y = 60k + 24$. But here $y < 60$, so we must have $k = 0$. Then the time was 1:24 A.M.
NOTE: See Appendix C.

82 HER SECRET

Say her age was X years, a 2-digit number. Then, $X + 11 = X/2 + 19$, whence $X = 16$. Barbara was 16 years old.

83 ONLY CANS

Say x at 49¢ and y at 39¢. Then $49x + 39y = 100x + y$, whence $51x = 38y$. But, y must be less than 100. So $x = 38$, and $y = 51$. They bought 38 at 49¢, 51 at 39¢.

84 UNEQUAL SHARES

$1/3 = 20/60$, $1/4 = 15/60$, $1/5 = 12/60$, $1/6 = 10/60$. So the division must be in proportions 20 to 15 to 12 to 10. The individual shares will be 20/57 of $14,934, i.e., $5240; 15/57, $3930; 12/57, $3144; 10/57, $2620. Doug would receive $2620.

85 THE DRIVE

Say d miles at 30 m.p.h. took $d/30$ hours, d miles at 36 m.p.h. took $d/36$ hours. Then $d(1/30 - 1/36) = 12/60 = 1/5$, whence $d = 36$. The distance was 36 miles.

86 GIVE AND TAKE

Say Stan had $3X$ cents, Martha $4Y$ cents.
Then, $2X + Y = 145$ and $3Y + X = 145$, whence $X = 58$, $Y = 29$. Stan had $1.74.

87 BIG BROTHER

Say Doug was $(x + y)$ years old, the other two ages being x and y years, and assume that $x \geq y$ (i.e., x equal to or greater than y). Then, $xy = 3(x + y)$, whence $xy - 3x - 3y = 0$, so $(x - 3)(y - 3) = 9$.

Tabulating for factors:

$x - 3$	$= 3$		9
$y - 3$	$= 3$		1
x	$= 6$		12
y	$= 6$		4

But we require $(x + y)$ as a "teenager," so $x + y = 16$. Doug was 16 years old.

88 ALIENS AT HOME

Say the price was X trigos a dozen, $144/X$ for 12 trigos. Then, at $(X - 1)$ trigos a dozen, he would have got $144/(X - 1)$ for 12 trigos. So $144/(X - 1) - 144/X = 2$, whence $X^2 - X - 72 = 0$, making $X = 9$. He bought 16 wrygans.

89 A LUCKY BREAK

Say X children, and each received $\$Y$ in bills.
Then $(402 - X)/X = XY$, so $402/X = XY + 1$. So X must be a factor of 402, i.e., of $2 \cdot 3 \cdot 67$. Ken had met 3 of the children, so $X > 2$, and obviously $X < 67$. Tabulate for possible values:

$X =$	3	6
$402/X =$	134	67
$XY =$	133	66
making $Y =$	—	11

There were 6 children. Having spent $\$6$ on mementos, the remaining $\$396$ was split into 6 portions of $\$66$ each, giving $\$11$ to each child.

90 TIES FOR DAD

Say prices: blue $3X$, green $4X$, the other tie Y cents. Then, $3X = (4X + Y)/3$, whence $Y = 5X$. So $12X =$

840, making $X = 35$. So prices were blue $2.10, green $2.80, and the other tie $3.50.

91 A PARADOX

Say the ages were: Mike x years, Betty y years.
Then, $x - 2 = 3(y - 2)$ and $x + 2 = 2(y + 2)$.
Thence $x - 3y = -4$ and $x - 2y = 2$, whence $x = 14, y = 6$.
Ages: Mike 14 years, Betty 6.

92 THE MOVE

When they moved, Stan was $6X$ years old, Susie X.
"Now," Stan is $(6X + 16)$ years old, Susie $(X + 16)$.
So, $6X + 16 = 2(X + 16)$, whence $X = 4$. At time of move, Susie was 4 years old.

93 ALL THE WAY FROM CHINA

Paying 329¢ a pound for x pounds oolong, and 238¢ a pound for y pounds lapsang, Sam had paid $(329x + 238y)$ cents. $(x + y)$ pounds at 448¢ a pound would come to $(448x + 448y)$ cents, giving a profit of $(119x + 210y)$ cents.
So, $119x + 210y = 60(329x + 238y)/100$, whence $7x = 6y$. Hence Sam's blend was 6 parts oolong to 7 parts lapsang souchong.

94 JUST IF

The digits are x, 4 and 6 in some order.
The initial digit cannot be 6, because $6 > 3$. It cannot be x, because the new number would still have initial digit x. So the initial digit is 4.
After the changes the new number must be even, to be divisible by 2, so its last digit cannot be 3 or 9. Hence the last digit must be x, and the digits in order must be $(4)(6)(x)$. Then $460 + x = (930 + x)/2 - 1$.
So $x = 8$.
The number is 468.

95   HE BROKE THE BANK

Say he had $x in bills, y¢ in coins. Then he had $(100x + y)$ cents. So, $100x/2 + 2y = 100x + y + 3$, whence $y = 50x + 3$, making $100x + y = 150x + 3$. He had "about three bucks," so $x = 2$, $y = 103$. In all, he had $3.03.

96   TAKE A CARD

Say Clive took $4x$ cards, leaving $(52 - 4x)$ on the table. Then he must have taken x blacks and $3x$ reds, leaving on the table $(26 - x)$ blacks and $(26 - 3x)$ reds.

After giving Clive 4 blacks, Mike had on the table $(48 - 4x)$ cards, $(26 - 3x)$ being red and $(22 - x)$ black.

Then, the odds must have been $(22 - x)$ to $(26 - 3x)$ against a red being drawn. So $(22 - x)/(26 - 3x) = 3$, whence $x = 7$. So Clive had taken 28 cards.

97   IT'S RELATIVE

Say her age was $(10X + Y)$. Then $10X + Y = 3XY$, whence $9XY - 30X - 3Y = 0$, hence $(3X - 1)(3Y - 10) = 10$.

Tabulate for factors, observing that X and Y are both single-digit integers:

$3X - 1 =$	10	5	2	1
$3Y - 10 =$	1	2	5	10
$X \;=$	—	2	1	—
$Y \;=$	—	4	5	—

Obviously the teacher's age would not be 15 years, so she was 24 years old.

98   FRESH FRUIT

He bought, say, x melons, $5x$ pears, y mangoes, $4y$ oranges. Then, $6x + 5y = 37$, whence $x = 2$, $y = 5$.

He had bought 2 melons, 5 mangoes, 10 pears, 20 oranges.

99 SOUVENIRS

Say Susan bought X cards, Harry $(X + 3)$. Then, $(2X + 3)$ cannot equal 12, so Harry's wife was Jane. Thence $(X + 3) + 2 = 12$, so $X = 7$. John bought 5 cards.

100 THE NUMBER MAN

The number was $(10x + y)$, say. Then, $5(x + 10y) - x - y = (10x + y)$, whence $6x = 48y$, making $x = 8y$. Thence we must have $x = 8$, with $y = 1$. The number was 81.

101 NOT HER PROBLEM

Each share would be worth 40¢.
Ron had paid 45¢ for what he had bought, so he should receive 5¢.
Bob had paid 75¢, so he should receive 35¢. Judy would pay 40¢ for her share of the candies.

102 NOT REALLY OLD

Say ages: Martin X years, Nancy Y years.
Then, $X - 3 = 4(Y - 3)$, whence $X - 4Y = -9$
....(A)
and $X + 3 = 3(Y + 3)$, whence $X - 3Y = 6$ ....(B)
Combining (A) and (B) we have $X = 51$, $Y = 15$.
Ages: Martin 51 years, Nancy 15.

103 ON THE ROAD

Say the bus speed is x m.p.h.
In 20 minutes the cyclists did 4 miles. Successive buses are $14x/60$, i.e., $7x/30$ miles apart. So in 20 minutes the 2nd bus would have done $(7x/30 + 4)$ miles. But that would be $x/3$ miles, so $7x + 120 = 10x$, $x = 40$. The bus speed was 40 m.p.h.

104   THIS OR THAT

Prices, say: print x cents, gilt frame $3y$ cents, black frame $2y$ cents. Then $x + 3y = 8775$, $x + 2y = 7500$, so $y = 1275$ with $x = 4950$. The price of the print alone was $49.50.

105   IN THE MIRROR

The clock appeared to show X hours and Y minutes. Then it really showed $(11 - X)$ hours and $(60 - Y)$ minutes.

But they had $X = 7$ and $Y = 12$. So the actual time was 4 hours and 48 minutes, i.e., 12 minutes before 5 o'clock.

106   LEAVE OF ABSENCE

If the period included February, then say there were X 31-day and $(6 - X)$ 30-day months, whence $31X + 30(6 - X) = 215 - 28$, or $215 - 29$, which makes $X = 7$ or 6. Impossible.

So February was not within the period, and we may say $31X + 30(7 - X) = 215$, whence $X = 5$. Hence the period was 5 31-day and 2 30-day months, so was July through January.

107   THE TESTS

Say $3n$ questions in each paper. In the first he got $(3n - 5)$ right, and $2n$ right in the second, so in all he had $(5n - 5)$ right. Thence, $(5n - 5)/6n = 3/4$, whence $n = 10$. There were 30 questions in each paper.

108   THEY'RE NOT THAT CHEAP NOW!

Say the candies were X cents a dozen. Then for $1 he would have got $1200/X$ candies.

If the price had been $(X - 5)$ cents a dozen, he would have got $1200/(X - 5)$.

So, $1200[1/(X - 5) - 1/X] = 8$, whence $X^2 - 5X - 750 = 0$. Hence, $X = 30$. So he got 40 candies for $1.

109   FIGURES, FIGURES

Say John's age was $(10x + y)$. Then $10x + y + x + y = 10y + x$, whence $5x = 4y$, so $x = 4$ with $y = 5$. John's age was 45.

110   DOLLARS AND CENTS

Say the price was $\$x$ and $y\cent$. Then $100x + y = 4y + 3x$, whence $97x = 3y$, so $x = 3, y = 97$. The price was $3.97.

111   A BUILDING LOT

The lot, say, was X by $(X + 40)$ feet, so $X(X + 40) = 9009$, whence $X^2 + 40X - 9009 = 0$, making $X = 77$. So the frontage was 77 feet.

112   IN THE BAG

Say Mike caught $2X$, Joe X, and Steve Y.

Then $2X = (X + Y)/4 + 1$, whence $Y = 7X - 4$. So their total was $(10X - 4)$, which was "about two dozen." That entailed $X = 3$, so Joe caught 3 fish.

113   FAIR'S FAIR

The price of each stamp was $42.

After allowing for the stamp that each man kept, their respective investments amounted to Eddie $14, Joe $28. So they should divide the $60 in that ratio, giving Eddie $20 and Joe $40.

114   NO SECRET

Age $(10x + y)$, say. Then, $(10x + y) - (x + y) = (10y + x)$. So, $8x = 10y$, whence $4x = 5y$. So $x = 5$, $y = 4$. The lady's age was 54 years.

115   THE WINNER

Say x first prizes, y second, $(12 - x - y)$ consolation prizes. Then, $2x + y + 3(12 - x - y)/4 = 13$, whence $5x + y = 16$. That has solutions $(x,y) = (3,1)$ or $(2,6)$ or $1,11$). But Jeff referred to prizes, so $y \neq 1$, and obviously $(x + y) \neq 12$. So we must have $x = 2$, with $y = 6$. There were 6 second prizes.

116   AT THE LUNCH COUNTER

Jim pays 82¢ less than his share, while Greg pays 45¢ more than his proper share. So Harry pays 37¢ more than his share, a total of $2.80 (i.e., $2.43 + 37¢). The total amount was $8.40.

117   AT THE CLUB

Mr. Tooth is neither dentist nor lawyer, so he is the painter. Then, the lawyer is not Mr. Law, so he is Mr. Painter. That leaves Mr. Law as the dentist.

118   A LITTLE OLD LADY

Say her age was $(10x + y)$ years. Then, $(10x + y - 10)/2 = 10y + x$, whence $8x - 19y = 10$, so $x = 6$, $y = 2$. Auntie Liz was 62 years old.

119   IT'S A FAKE

Mark the coins 1 through 8.
Weigh 1, 2, 3 against 4, 5, 6. If they balance, then weigh 7 against 8 to determine the heavier coin. If the initial trios do not balance, then weigh any one coin from the heavy trio against another from the same trio, and that will determine the heavier coin.

120   PROGRESS

Say there were X girls, Y men. Then, $2X + Y = 30$, and $X + 3Y = 30$. Thence, $X = 12$, $Y = 6$. There were 18 clerks in all.

121   WIN OR LOSE

Say Peter won x games, Jack won y, 2 games were drawn. Then, $x + 2 = (x + y + 2)/2$, and $y + 2 = 2(x + y + 2)/3$. Thence, $x - y = -2$, and $2x - y = 2$, so $x = 4$, $y = 6$. They had played 12 games, and Peter won 4.

122   A RURAL SCENE

Say $5X$ cows standing and $4Y$ lying down to start with. Then, after John honked there were $(4X + Y)$ standing and $(3Y + X)$ lying down.
So, $4X + Y = X + 3Y$, whence $3X = 2Y$. Thence $4Y = 6X$, making $5X + 4Y = 11X$. But the total was "about 20," so $X = 2$, and there were 22 cows in all.

123   MALE CHAUVINISTS

Say $4x$ girls and $3x$ boys.
If 7 more boys, there would have been $(3x + 7)$ boys. So, $(3x + 7)/4x = 4/3$, whence $x = 3$. There were 12 girls and 9 boys at the party.

124 SUBSCRIPTIONS

Say X contributions were listed prior to Jack's. Then the total had been $222X$ cents.

So, $222X + 1400 = 241(X + 1)$, making $X = 61$.

Hence the total had been $(222 \cdot 61)$, i.e., 13542 cents.

Jack's \$14 brought the total up to \$149.42.

125 A NEW NUMBER

Say the digits, in that order, were y, x, x, x^2. Then $x^2 + 2x + y = 23$.

We have $y < 10$, so $x^2 + 2x > 13$, making $x > 2$. Also, since y could be 0, $x^2 + 2x < 24$, making $x < 4$.

So $x = 3$, with $y = 8$. The number was 8339.

126 WHO WANTS A SQUARE?

Say the patio had been X feet square, with area X^2 square feet. Then, $(X + 4)(X - 3) = X^2 + 1$, making $X = 13$. The new dimensions were 17 feet by 10 feet.

127 IT MAKES SENSE

(See detailed solution to No. 72, "Strange but True.")

Say the numeration system is base n.

"Nine times ten" is ninety. So, $n^2 + 3n + 2 = 90$, whence $n = 8$.

Then, working in our usual base-10 system, we would have $9 \cdot 5 = 45 = 5 \cdot 8 + 5$. In the base-8 system that would be written as 55 and read in words as "five five," not "fifty-five."

128 THEY MET AGAIN

Say the ages were: Ted x, the girls $(x - y)$ and $(x + y)$ years. Then, $x^2 = 2[(x + y)^2 - (x - y)^2] =$

$8xy$, so $x = 8y$, making the ages: Ted $8y$, and the girls $7y$ and $9y$ years.

6 years previously the ages had been: Ted ($8y - 6$), and the girls ($7y - 6$) and ($9y - 6$) years.

So, $(8y - 6)^2 = 3[(9y - 6)^2 - (7y - 6)^2]/2$, whence $4y^2 - 15y + 9 = 0$, making integral $y = 3$.

The ages were: Ted 24, and the girls 21 and 27 years.

129 A MATTER OF FOURS

Say Mac had \$$x$ in bills, y¢ in coins, a total of ($100x + y$) cents. Then, with \$4 more in bills and 4¢ less in coins, he would have $[100(x + 4) + (y - 4)]$ cents.

So, $100(x + 4) + y - 4 = 3(100x + y)$, whence $y = 198 - 100x$, making $x = 1$, with $y = 98$. He had \$1.98.

130 WHAT? US?

Say Jill's age was ($10X + Y$) years.

Then Tony's age was ($10 \cdot 2Y + 2X$) years, so $2X + 20Y = 10X + Y + 6$, whence $19Y - 8X = 6$, with general integral solution $Y = 8k + 2$. Obviously we must have $k = 0$ here, so $Y = 2$, with $X = 4$. Jill's age was 42 years, Tony's 48.

NOTE: See Appendix C.

131 THE HANDICAP

Say Betty's step was $4x$ units, Bill's $5x$ units. Then Betty had a $40x$-unit "start."

Bill ran $5y$ steps, say, a distance of $25xy$ units, while Betty ran $6y$ steps, a distance of $24xy$ units. So $25xy = 24xy + 40x$, whence $y = 40$. Bill ran 200 steps.

132   THE MORNING AFTER

Say X cigars remained in the box after Kim had taken 1 cigar. Then, they had smoked $(50 - 1 - X)$.

So, $2(49 - X) = X/2 + 3$, whence $X = 38$. Hence, 38 cigars remained.

133   SHARE AND SHARE ALIKE

Sharing the candies three ways, each share was worth 35¢, the amount Betty had to pay.

Steve had paid 45¢, so was entitled to a refund of 10¢. Ken had paid 60¢, so was entitled to a refund of 25¢.

134   LONG, LONG AGO

Say X days in the month prior to the date, and $6X$ days after it. Then that month had $(7X + 1)$ days, so must have been a Leap Year February with 29 days.

The only Leap Year in the 1914/18 period was the year 1916. So that special date was 5 February 1916.

135   FOR A GOOD CAUSE

Say there were $3x$ women and $(88 - 3x)$ men.

Then women gave $(94 \cdot 2x)$ cents, and men gave $50(88 - 3x)$ cents. Thence, $188x + 4400 - 150x = 5084$, making $x = 18$.

So there were 54 women and 34 men, whence 17 men contributed.

136   MERCHANDISING

Say Dan bought the belts at x cents each.

Profit on the first 26 was $26(695 - x)$ cents, profit on the next 55 was $55(499 - x)$ cents.

Thence, $55(499 - x) - 26(695 - x) = 675$, so $x = 300$. Dan had paid $3.00 each.

137 JUST FIGURES

Say the number has digits $(X)(Y)$ in that order. Then $10X + Y = Z^3 + 3$, say. But, $Y = 13 - X$, so $9X = Z^3 - 10$.

Obviously, $Z > 2$. $9X < 82$, so $Z < 5$. If $Z = 3$, we have $9X = 17$, not divisible by 9. But $4^3 - 10 = 6 \cdot 9$, so $X = 6$, with $Y = 7$. The number was 67.

138 SORT THAT ONE OUT

Say ages were: Judy x, Mike $(x + y)$ years.
Work back from comma:
When Mike was x, Judy was $(x - y)$.
When Mike was $3(x - y)$, July was $(3x - 4y)$.
When Mike was $2(3x - 4y)$, Judy was $(6x - 9y)$.
Now work back from end of paragraph:
When Judy was $(x + y)/2$, Mike was $(x + 3y)/2$.
Half that is $(x + 3y)/4$.

So, $(x + 3y)/4 = 6x - 9y$, whence $23x = 39y$, which entails $x = 39k$, $y = 23k$ and $(x + y) = 62k$. Obviously we must have $k = 1$, making Mike's age 62 years, and Judy's 39 years.

139 THE GIRLS NEXT DOOR

Say Ann was in blue, with Eve in red. Then, since Carol and Eve do not wear the same color, Carol would be in blue. But Carol and Ann cannot both be in blue.

So Ann was in red; with Carol in red and Eve in blue.

140 THE BIRD LOVER

The previous week there were X finches, say.
The old lady left $(2X - 1)/3$.
The kids left $(4X - 5)/9 = 11$, so $X = 26$.
The old lady took $26/3 + 1/3$, i.e., 9 finches.

141   A BAD YEAR

Say x trees. Then, $97x = x^2 - 3500$, so $x^2 - 97x - 3500 = 0$, whence $x = 125$. There were 125 trees.

142   FRACTIONS

Say X candies.
Then the kids had $X/3 + X/4 + X/5 + X/6$, a total of $57X/60$. Betty had 6, so $3X/60 = 6$, whence $X = 120$. There were 120 candies.

143   WAITING

Say the time was $5x$ minutes after noon, so $(420 - 5x)$ minutes before 7:00 P.M. Hence $(420 - 5x)/4 + x = 5x$, making $x = 20$, $5x = 100$. The time was 1:40 P.M.

144   VACATION TIME

Don did not go to Tulla or Brent, so he went to Skerrig.
Harry did not go to Tulla, so he went to Brent. Hence the third boy went to Tulla.

145   NO CHILDREN

Say, X married men, X married women, Y single women, and 5 single men. Then, $2X + Y + 5 = 37$, whence $2X + Y = 32$, and $X + Y = 20$. So $X = 12$. There were 12 married men at the meeting.

146   THE OLD HOME

Say the ages were: Dad, x years; Fred, y years; house, $\sqrt{(100x + y)} = x + 15$. Thence, $x^2 + 30x + 225 = 100x + y$, whence $y = x^2 - 70x +$

$225 = (x - 35)^2 - 1000$. Now, $y < 100$, so $(x - 35)$ = 32 or 33.

With $(x - 35) = 33$, we would have $x = 68$, $y = 89$. But obviously $x > y$, so $(x - 35) = 32$, making $x = 67$, with $y = 24$. Then, $6724 = 82^2$.

The house was 82 years old.

147 MENTAL ARITHMETIC

Say the number was X. Then, $300003 + 10X = 43X$, so $33X = 300003$, whence $X = 9091$.

148 SHE FORGOT

We have, say, $N = x^2 + 19 = y^2 - 18$. Then, $y^2 - x^2 = 37$.

So, $(y + x)(y - x) = 37$, making $y = 19$ with $x = 18$. Hence, the number was 343.

149 THREE IN A ROW

Say the number had digits $(x)(y)(z)$ in that order, with value $(100x + 10y + z)$. The stated changes would give a new value $(430 + z)$.

Thence, $100x + 10y + z = 860 + 2z$, so $100x + 10y - z = 860$, making $x = 8$. That leads to $10y - z = 60$, so $z = 0$. Hence the number was 860.

150 RIDING SCHOOL

Say, X horses, Y humans. Thence, $(X + Y)$ heads, X tails, $(4x + 2Y)$ feet. So, $4x + 2Y = X + Y + 40$, and $X + Y = X + 13$. Hence, $Y = 13$, $X = 9$. There were 9 horses.

151 MORE TRAINS

Say the prices were \$$x$ and \$$y$, with $x > y$.

Then, $2x + y = 32$, and $x + 2y = 28$. So $x = 12$, $y = 8$. The prices were \$12 and \$8.

152   1066 AND ALL THAT

The boy was born in a year that was a multiple of 17. The battle was in 1066, so he was born a few years before that year, $1054 = 17 \cdot 62$, making him 12 years old at the battle if born in that year. If born in 1037, however, he would have been 29 years old for the battle, not a "young boy."

Hence he was born in 1054, and died in the year 1116 at the age of 62 years.

153   A MATTER OF TIME

Say the time was X hours and Y minutes. The hour hand would be at $(60X + Y)/12$ minutes, $[60 - (60X + Y)/12]$ minutes before twelve o'clock: the minute hand at $(Y - 30)$ minutes after the half hour.

So, $(Y - 30) = 6[60 - (60X + Y)/12]$, whence $Y + 20X = 260$. But X is an integer, so $X = 11$, $Y = 40$. It was obviously daytime, so the time was 11:40 A.M.

154   THE RENDEZVOUS

Judy drove x miles, say, at 42 m.p.h., in $x/42$ hours. Don drove $(x + 3)$ miles at 56 m.p.h., in $(x + 3)/56$ hours.

So, $x/42 - (x + 3)/56 = 1/3$, whence $x = 65$. Don drove 68 miles.

155   WOT? NO CRYSTAL?

Say X larger glasses at 97¢, Y smaller at 59¢. Then, $59Y - 97X = 50$, with general solution $X = 59k + 8$, $Y = 97k + 14$. But Ann had paid less than \$20, so here we must have $k = 0$. Then she bought 8 of the larger and 14 of the smaller glasses.
NOTE: See Appendix C.

156 AT THE PUMPS

Say x 8-cylinder, y 6-cylinder, $2y$ 4-cylinder.
Then, $8x + 6y + 8y = 74$, whence $4x + 7y = 37$, with general solution $y = 4k + 3$. But $7y < 37$, so $y = 3$, with $x = 4$. Hence there were 4 8-cylinder cars.

157 THE REC ROOM

Either size of tiles would fit exactly, so say the dimensions of the room were $36X$ by $36Y$ inches. Then the floor area was $1296XY$ square inches.
That would require $16XY$ 9-inch tiles at 19¢, for $304XY$ cents. It would require $9XY$ 12-inch tiles at 29¢, for $261XY$ cents.
So, $304XY - 261XY = 3311$, making $XY = 77 = 7 \cdot 11$. Obviously, $Y = 1$ would not be acceptable, so $X = 11, Y = 7$. The floor was 33 feet by 21 feet.

158 NEARLY BROKE

Jack had, say, X dimes and Y pennies, total value $(10X + Y)$ cents. With the dimes as nickels and the pennies as quarters, the total value would be $(5X + 25Y)$ cents.
So, $5X + 25Y = 10X + Y + 100$, whence $(24Y - 5X) = 100$. But Jack had less than \$2 in all, so Y, which must be 5 or some multiple of 5, had to be 5, with $X = 4$. Then Jack had 4 dimes and 5 pennies, a total of 45¢.

159 THE QUESTION

Say Aunt Amelia's age had digits $(x)(y)$ in that order. Then, $10y + x = (10x + y - 5)/3$, whence $7x - 29y = 5$. So, $x = 9$, with $y = 2$. The lady was 92 years old.

160   THE TRAIN BUFFS

Say the distance from Cove to Tulla was d miles, the distance from Brent to Cove $2d$ miles. Their train's speed was $5x$ m.p.h., the other's train's speed $4x$ m.p.h.

Their train took $2d/5x$ hours to reach Cove, the other train took $d/4x$ hours. So, $d/4x = 2d/5x - 1$, whence $3d = 20x$.

Their time for the further stretch, Cove to Tulla, would be $d/5x$. But $d = 20x/3$, so they would take $5/3$ hours, i.e., 1 hour and 20 minutes to reach Tulla.

ALPHAMETICS

ALPHAMETICS

It all started thousands of years ago, probably in ancient China, with puzzles in which the numerals of arithmetical calculations were replaced by letters or other symbols. In such puzzles, known centuries ago as "letter arithmetic" and more recently as "cryptarithms," distinct digits were represented by particular but different letters, the solver being required to reconstruct the original numerical layouts. A very simple example would be:

$$
\begin{array}{ccc}
 & P & K \\
 & K & N \\
\hline
K & N & K
\end{array}
$$

In 1955 I coined a new word "alphametic" to designate a more sophisticated and more interesting-looking variation on the theme. In an alphametic the letters must form meaningful words in meaningful phrases instead of the jumbled array of the cryptarithm. As an alphametic, then, the puzzle shown above could appear as:

$$
\begin{array}{ccc}
 & A & D \\
 & D & I \\
\hline
D & I & D
\end{array}
\qquad \text{with unique solution} \qquad
\begin{array}{ccc}
 & 9 & 1 \\
 & 1 & 0 \\
\hline
1 & 0 & 1
\end{array}
$$

This is *meaningful* as referring to an advertisement that Diana produced. Although precisely the same problem arithmetically, the alphametic has a form that is obviously more likely to arouse the interest of ordinary people who might well be repelled by the apparently meaningless "jumbled letters" form. In fact, the introduction of the alphametic and its acceptance by puzzlemakers throughout the world have led to an amazing spread of popular interest in this form as a pastime that requires only basic arithmetical understanding and sound reasoning for its enjoyment.

In the forty alphametics that follow these introductory remarks only addition and multiplication are involved. More difficult alphametics can be constructed, however, based on other arithmetical processes and even on the solution of differential equations.

Detailed *solutions* for the first two of our alphametics are given in the Solutions section to show the sort of approach that leads to a satisfactory conclusion, but only the bare *answers* are given for the others.

No two alphametics, even of the same type, require the same approach. It is quite impossible to lay down any specific rules or routines for solving such puzzles. However, a few observations and hints of a general nature may help the reader who is not familiar with this popular pastime.

The first essential, then, after copying the layout onto a sheet of paper, is to study the letters of the alphametic and write down any obvious facts regarding their relationships. In doing this the solver may adopt a special symbol that can save space. If we multiply 3 by 4, the product *ends in* 2. Instead of that rather long sentence, the same fact can be noted as "3 × 4 → 2." Similarly, 24 × 19 → 6, and even 24 × 19 → 56. This is a most useful device, and it will be seen in the first detailed solution that follows.

Among the points that may be involved when solving an alphametic, all within the framework of simple arithmetic, the following are worth noting here.

(a) Say we have one "column" in an addition or

subtraction appearing as $\dfrac{\begin{array}{c}K\\K\end{array}}{K}$, then we know that

K is zero *or* 9. The possibility of a "carry" or "borrow" being involved in such cases must always be considered. A somewhat similar situation arises

where, say, "K + K + T + carry → T" entailing
"K + K + carry → zero."
(b) No perfect square can end with 2, 3, 7 or 8.
For example, say we have (E × E) → G. Then G
cannot represent 2, 3, 7 or 8. Also, since 5^2 → 5,
6^2 → 6, and 1^2 → 1, in such a case we would be
limited to the following pairs of values, which
could be written down as known facts:

$$E = 2 \quad 3 \quad 4 \quad 7 \quad 9$$
$$G = 4 \quad 9 \quad 6 \quad 9 \quad 1$$

(c) When carrying out a regular arithmetical cal-
culation, we never write down a zero as the *first*
digit of a number. Hence in an alphametic, the
initial letter of a "word" can never stand for zero.

The forty alphametics are graded very approxi-
mately according to difficulty, but they are all quite
easy.

PROBLEMS

1
```
    T U T
    T U T
        A
  -------
    R A T
```

2
```
        N O
      G U N
        N O
  ---------
    H U N T
```

3
```
    A D A M
    A D A M
      I ' M
          A
  ---------
  M I S S
```
Of course he'd never seen
one before!

4   In this multiplication the
little "x's" stand for digits
that you'll have to identify.
```
        G O
        O N
  ---------
        x x
      x x x
  ---------
    T R O T
```

5
```
  D A D
  H A D
      A
─────────
H I F I
```

6
```
R A C E
  F A N
  C A N
─────────
C H E E R
```

7 A number is prime if it can be divided without remainder only by itself and by unity. This FROG is truly prime!
```
G L U G
G L U G
F R O G
─────────
G U L P S
```

8
```
  A N N
  A N N
      A
─────────
P L A N
```

9
```
  S I S
  S I S
  I T' S
─────────
T H I S
```

10
```
  L E T' S
    S E E
        A
─────────
T O T A L
```

11
```
  B O B
  B O B
  D O
─────────
L O O K
```

12
```
S P O T
  T H E
B E S T
─────────
S P O T S
```

13
```
L O T S
S O L D
    T O
  O L D
─────────
F O O L S
```

14
```
      N O
  M O O N
      N O
  C A N
─────────
S P O O N
```

15
```
  W O W
  W H A T
        A
─────────
T O O T
```

16

```
    B O N G
    B O N G
    B O N G
  ─────────
  G O N G S
```

17 Dogs often die from eating them! Indeed, TOADS must be truly odd.

```
    D O G S
    D O G S
      N O
  ─────────
  T O A D S
```

18

```
  T A K E
        A
  C A K E
  ───────
  K A T E
```

19

```
  A D A M
  A N D
  E V E
  ───────
  M O V E D
```

20

```
    G O T
  L O O T
    G O T
  ───────
  G O L D
```

21

```
  A L A S
        A
  L A M E
  ───────
  C A M E L
```

22

```
  D A D
  H A D
      A
  B A D
  ─────
  H E A D
```

23

```
  M U M M Y
  M U M M Y
      M Y
  ─────────
  Y O G U R T
```

24

```
      S E E
  A R A B S
  R A C E
  ─────────
  B A R B S
```

25

```
  R A M A
  M E T
        A
  T A M E
  ───────
  T I G E R
```

26
```
Y U M M Y
Y U M M Y
    I N
    M Y
---------
T U M M Y
```

27
```
F A T S O
  E A T S
  M O S T
S W E E T
-----------
S W E E T S
```

28
```
S N I F F
S N I F F
  P R I M
---------
M I S S E S
```

29
```
    B A A
    B A A
        A
---------
L A M B
```

30
```
S H U S H
S H U S H
    N O
---------
N O I S E
```

31
```
  H E A R
T H O S E
T H R E E
---------
C H E E R S
```

32
```
  A N T S
  M A D E
T A P I R
  A N T
---------
D I N N E R
```

33
```
H A N D Y
  A N D Y
  H A D
      A
---------
D A N D Y
S E D A N
```

34
```
        N O
R A I N S
    N O
R A I N S
    O N
-----------
S A H A R A
```

35
```
  Z A N Y
Z E B R A
R A Z E D
---------
Z A R E B A
```

36
```
      S A L L Y
      S E L L S
        D A D' S
  ─────────────
  A P P L E S
```

37
```
        A H O Y
        A H O Y
      T H E R E
          A L L
  ─────────────
  A B O A R D
```

38
```
        I C E
      N I C E
        I   N
        G I N
    ───────────
    S L I N G
```

39
```
    P E T E' S
      T E N T
          N O
      N E A T
    ───────────
    T E P E E
```

40
```
      N E R O
        N   O
      H E R O
        T   O
    ───────────
    R O M A N
```

SOLUTIONS TO ALPHAMETICS

SOLUTIONS TO ALPHAMETICS

1
```
  T U T
  T U T
      A
  ─────
  R A T
```
From the TTAT column we have $T + A = 10$, giving "carry 1." Then, from "U + U," A must be odd, with T also odd. But obviously $T < 5$ (i.e., "less than 5"), so tabulate possible values, avoiding duplications:

$$
\begin{array}{rccc}
& T & = & 1 \quad 3 \\
\text{with} & A & = & 9 \quad 7 \\
\hline
U + & U & \rightarrow & 8 \quad 6 \\
\text{whence} & U & = & 4 \quad 8 \\
\text{with} & R & = & 2 \quad - \\
\end{array}
$$

So we have $141 + 141 + 9 = 291$.
(NOTE: $\rightarrow$ means "ends with.")

2
```
    N O
  G U N
    N O
  ─────
H U N T
```
Obviously $H = 1$. From the NUNN column we must have "carry 1," so $G = 9$, $U = $ zero. Since we have "carry" zero or 1 or 2 from the ONOT column, correspondingly we have $N + U = 10$ or 9 or 8. But duplication is not allowed, so $N = 8$ with "carry 2" from ONOT. Hence, $O + O = T + 20 - 8 = T + 12$. Testing for $T = 2$, 4 or 6, we find only $T = 2$ acceptable, $O = 7$. So we have $87 + 908 + 87 = 1082$.

3	$1813 + 1813 + 73 + 1 = 3700.$
4	$27 \times 73 = 1971.$
5	$929 + 129 + 2 = 1060.$
6	$9715 + 672 + 172 = 10559.$
7	$1521 + 1521 + 9461 = 12503.$
8	$733 + 733 + 7 = 1473.$
9	$585 + 585 + 815 = 1985.$
10	$9615 + 566 + 8 = 10189.$
11	$757 + 757 + 45 = 1559.$
12	$1029 + 943 + 8319 = 10291.$
13	$5478 + 8453 + 74 + 453 = 14458.$
14	$62 + 9226 + 62 + 876 = 10226.$
15	$101 + 1892 + 9 = 2002.$
16	$7142 + 7142 + 7142 = 21426.$
17	$8743 + 8743 + 97 = 17583.$
18	$3961 + 9 + 2961 = 6931.$
19	$8581 + 875 + 939 = 10395.$
20	$516 + 4116 + 516 = 5148.$
21	$4947 + 4 + 9438 = 14389.$
22	$848 + 248 + 4 + 948 = 2048.$
23	$90991 + 90991 + 91 = 182073.$
24	$155 + 26231 + 6245 = 32631.$
25	$7949 + 481 + 9 + 1948 = 10387.$
26	$29882 + 29882 + 36 + 82 = 59882.$
27	$83412 + 7341 + 6214 + 10774 = 107741.$
28	$79633 + 79633 + 8461 = 167727.$
29	$622 + 622 + 2 = 1246.$
30	$34534 + 34534 + 69 = 69137.$
31	$2785 + 62397 + 62577 = 127759.$
32	$7289 + 6713 + 87504 + 728 = 102234.$
33	$23465 + 3465 + 236 + 3 + 63465 = 90634.$
34	$47 + 50941 + 47 + 50941 + 74 = 102050.$
35	$1074 + 18590 + 90186 = 109850.$
36	$61884 + 69886 + 2126 = 133896.$
37	$1824 + 1824 + 98373 + 155 = 102176.$
38	$538 + 9538 + 59 + 459 = 10594.$
39	$74843 + 8418 + 15 + 1468 = 84744$ (3, 5 interchangeable).
40	$8217 + 87 + 9217 + 47 = 17568.$

APPENDICES

APPENDICES

APPENDIX A

The simplest type of equation is called a *linear equation*.

Mentally, and probably without realizing that they are doing so, most people solve equations of this type every day. Maybe you bought seven pears for sixty-three cents. What did each cost? "In your head," you divided 63 by 7, deriving 9¢ per pear. In fact, you virtually said $7X = 63$, so $X = 63/7 = 9$.

Where we have two (or three or more) equations of this type, all applying simultaneously, the operation is not quite so simple.

Say we have $5X + 3Y = 36$ and $2X + 7Y = 55$. The standard approach to such a "pair of simultaneous equations" is to eliminate X or Y, as shown here:

Multiplying the first by 2, we derive

$$10X + 6Y = 72.$$

Multiplying the second by 5, we derive

$$10X + 35Y = 275.$$

Subtracting one from the other, so

$$29Y = 203.$$
$$Y = 7.$$

Then, from the first equation, we have $5X = 36 - 21 = 15$, so $X = 3$.

It will be noted that we can multiply each side of an equation by the same number without destroying the equality. So in this case we chose to multiply each side of one equation by 2, and each side of the other by 5, in order to arrive at identical coefficients for X (i.e., 10): that enabled us to eliminate the X terms by subtraction.

The same principle is used in solving a system of three or more simultaneous equations. For example, say we have:

$$\left. \begin{array}{l} 2X + 3Y - 2Z = 15 \\ 3X + \ Y + \ Z = 16 \\ \ X + 4Y + 3Z = 19 \end{array} \right\} \begin{array}{l} \text{(A)} \\ \text{(B)} \\ \text{(C)} \end{array}$$

Here it will be convenient to eliminate the Z terms first.

Multiplying equation (B) by 2 and by 3, we can set up two pairs of valid equations:

$$\left. \begin{array}{l} 2X + 3Y - 2Z = 15 \\ 6X + 2Y + 2Z = 32 \end{array} \right\}$$

Eliminating Z, $\quad 8X + 5Y \qquad = 47$

and

$$\left. \begin{array}{l} 9X + 3Y + 3Z = 48 \\ \ X + 4Y + 3Z = 19 \end{array} \right\}$$

Eliminating Z, $\quad 8X - \ Y \qquad = 29$

Now we have the pair of simultaneous equations:

$$\left. \begin{array}{l} 8X + 5Y = 47 \\ 8X - \ Y = 29 \end{array} \right\}$$

Eliminating X, $\qquad\qquad 6Y = 18;$ whence $Y = 3.$

Then, substituting this value for Y, we have $8X = 32$, so $X = 4$.

Finally, we substitute these values for X and Y, in equation (B), to derive $Z = 16 - 12 - 3 = 1$. So $X = 4, Y = 3, Z = 1$.

APPENDIX B

A *quadratic equation* involves the square of the "unknown."

The standard solution for this type of equation, derived in detail and proved in any elementary algebra textbook, is not difficult to remember:
If $ax^2 - bx + c = 0$, then $2ax = b \pm \sqrt{b^2 - 4ac}$.

In many cases, however, a rather different approach is preferable, although it of course leads to the same ultimate result. This entails no formula to be remembered and should be quite easy to understand from a couple of numerical examples. It will be seen that we manipulate the equation as necessary in order to transform it into a new equation of form $X^2 = Y$, which must have two solutions: $X = +\sqrt{Y}$ and $X = -\sqrt{Y}$.

Say we have $x^2 + x - 12 = 0$. Multiplying by 4, this becomes $4x^2 + 4x - 48 = 0$, which can be shown as $4x^2 + 4x + 1 = 49$. Then $(2x + 1)^2 = 49$, so $2x + 1 = \pm 7$; whence $x = 3$ **or** $x = -4$.

In a more complex example, say $3x^2 - 19x - 14 = 0$, multiplying by 12, this becomes $36x^2 - 228x - 168 = 0$, which can be shown as $36x^2 - 228x + 361 = 529$. Then $(6x - 19)^2 = 529$, so $6x - 19 = \pm 23$; whence $x = 7$ **or** $x = -2/3$.

APPENDIX C

Many popular teasers depend on the solution of what is called a *simple indeterminate equation,* a very simple example of which would be the equation $7X - 3Y = 11$ with the stipulation that X and Y must both be whole numbers.

That *whole number* condition is inherent in such equations, and is vital in solving them.

Say we wish to solve $7X - 3Y = 11$, where X and Y are both whole numbers.

Since 3 is the smaller of the two coefficients, we divide through by 3:

$$2X + \frac{X}{3} - Y = 4 - \frac{1}{3}$$

which becomes $\dfrac{X + 1}{3} = Y - 2X + 4$

Now $(Y - 2X + 4)$ must be a whole number, so $\dfrac{X + 1}{3}$ must be a whole number.

Say $\dfrac{X + 1}{3} = k$, where k is some unspecified whole number (positive, negative, or even zero). Then $X = 3k - 1$.

Substituting this value for X in the original equation, we have $3Y = 21k - 18$; whence $Y = 7k - 6$.

The general solution, then, is $X = 3k - 1$, $Y = 7k - 6$.

By giving any desired whole-number value to k, we will obtain a particular numerical solution to the original equation. For example, with $k = 2$, we have $X = 5, Y = 8$.

Where a popular teaser involves solution of such an equation, there will be some extra condition to pinpoint the required particular solution among the infinite number of possible whole-number solutions. In our example, we might have some stipulation that required Y to be "in the thirties"; then we should have to set $k = 6$, giving $X = 17, Y = 36$.

This was a very simple example. When we divided through by 3, the coefficient of Y, we obtained the fraction of X as $X/3$: a fraction with unity as numerator (as opposed to $2X/3$, say).

So now we consider a slightly more complex case, taking the equation $11X - 7Y = 2$.

Dividing through by 7, the smaller coefficient as before, we have $X + \dfrac{4X}{7} - Y = \dfrac{2}{7}$; whence $\dfrac{4X - 2}{7}$ is a whole number, so $\dfrac{2(2X - 1)}{7}$ is a whole number.

Then $\dfrac{2X - 1}{7}$ must be a whole number.

Here we do not have unity as the coefficient of X in the numerator of the fraction, so we must take a further step to arrive at that necessary situation.

If we multiply a whole number by any whole number, the result will be a whole number. So we multiply by a selected whole number, such that the new coefficient of X will be "1 more" (or "1 less") than a multiple of 7. For this we select 4 as our multiplier.

Multiplying by 4, $\dfrac{2X - 1}{7}$ becomes $\dfrac{8X - 4}{7}$, which will also be a whole number. That, in turn, becomes $X + \dfrac{X - 4}{7}$, which implies that $\dfrac{X - 4}{7}$ must be a whole number.

Now we have unity as the coefficient of X in the numerator, so we can say $\dfrac{X - 4}{7} = k$; whence $X = 7k + 4$. Then, substituting this value for X in the original equation (i.e., $11X - 7Y = 2$), we derive $Y = 11k + 6$.

The required general solution, then, is $X = 7k + 4$, $Y = 11k + 6$.

If some condition stipulated that X in this case must be between 40 and 50, we would have to set $k = 6$, giving $X = 46$, $Y = 72$.

The selection of the right *multiplier* is sometimes far from easy (in this last example, 4 could be picked at sight). In such cases it may have to be found by a process of trial, bearing in mind the desired result. There is a standard method for calculating what the *multiplier* should be, without trial and error, and this will be found in textbooks, but the principles involved are somewhat outside the scope of this book.

APPENDIX D

Many of the more difficult popular teasers entail the solving of what are called *second-degree indeterminate equations,* which may be described more simply as indeterminate equations that involve squares. A simple example is $3x^2 + 2xy - y^2 = 15$, in which, as in all indeterminate equations, we are concerned only with whole-number values of x and y.

We take that example, writing it as $3x^2 + 2yx - y^2 - 15 = 0$, and treat this as an ordinary quadratic equation in x (see Appendix B).

Then $6x = -2y \pm \sqrt{4y^2 + 12y^2 + 180}$;

whence $3x = -y \pm \sqrt{4y^2 + 45}$ .... (A)

Since whole-number values are required, the expression under the square-root sign must be a perfect square. This, or some similar requirement, is basic in the solution of most second-degree indeterminate equations.

So say $4y^2 + 45 = k^2$, whence k is some unspecified whole number.

Then $k^2 - (2y)^2 = 45$; whence $(k + 2y)(k - 2y) = 45$.

We now tabulate, bringing in the possible pairs of factors of 45, but observing that with a positive value of y we must have $(k + 2y)$ greater than $(k - 2y)$, for negative values are unlikely to be called for in a popular teaser.

$k + 2y$ =		45	15	9
$k - 2y$ =		1	3	5
adding gives				
k =		23	9	7
subtracting gives				
y =		11	3	1
from (A)				
$3x$ =		12 or -34	6 or -12	6 or -8
whence				
x =		4	—	2 or -4	2	—

We disregarded fractional values of x in the last line of the tabulation. Assuming we seek only positive values for x and y, we have found that there are three acceptable solutions:

$x = 4, y = 11;\ x = 2, y = 3;\ x = 2, y = 1.$

We now take a rather less simple example, in which the same principles will be seen to apply.

Say $x^3 - 3xy - 7y = 11$, both x and y being positive.

Then $x^2 - 3yx - 7y - 11 = 0$, which has solution in x: $2x = 3y \pm \sqrt{(9y^2 + 28y + 44)}$............(B)

So $9y^2 + 28y + 44 = k^2$ (compare with previous example), and $81y^2 + 252y + 396 = 9k^2$; hence $(9y + 14)^2 + 200 = 9k^2$. so $(3k)^2 - (9y + 14)^2 = 200$.

Here $(9y + 14)$ must obviously be positive, so we tabulate for three alternative pairs of factors of 200; i.e., $[3k + (9y + 14)][3k - (9y + 14)] = 100 \times 2$, or 50×4, or 20×10.

Carrying through the tabulation procedure, as in the previous example, and using the solution given in (B), only one acceptable solution will be found in positive whole numbers: $x = 6$, $y = 1$.

It should be noted that in both examples we arrived at a final stage with a modified equation in the form $X^2 - Y^2 = m$, where m is a whole number.

In almost all second-degree indeterminate equations the solution depends on deriving a modified equation in the form $X^2 \pm eY^2 = m$. In the two examples already considered, the e was unity and the minus sign applied. In many cases, the e will be some whole number other than unity, with either plus or minus sign, and the whole number m may be negative; for example $(x + 1)^2 + 2k^2 = 83$, $(2y - 3)^2 - 3k^2 = -83$, etc.

This brief introduction, however, can be no place for further discussion of those and other more complex cases: they are all covered in detail in textbooks, and some special aspects are discussed at length in *Mathematical Diversions*, by J. A. H. Hunter and J. S. Madachy. What has been outlined here may have introduced the reader to the general principles that are involved in dealing with second-degree indeterminate equations.

A CATALOG OF SELECTED
DOVER BOOKS
IN ALL FIELDS OF INTEREST

A CATALOG OF SELECTED
DOVER BOOKS
IN ALL FIELDS OF INTEREST

DRAWINGS OF REMBRANDT, edited by Seymour Slive. Updated Lippmann, Hofstede de Groot edition, with definitive scholarly apparatus. All portraits, biblical sketches, landscapes, nudes. Oriental figures, classical studies, together with selection of work by followers. 550 illustrations. Total of 630pp. 9⅛ × 12¼.
21485-0, 21486-9 Pa., Two-vol. set $29.90

GHOST AND HORROR STORIES OF AMBROSE BIERCE, Ambrose Bierce. 24 tales vividly imagined, strangely prophetic, and decades ahead of their time in technical skill: "The Damned Thing," "An Inhabitant of Carcosa," "The Eyes of the Panther," "Moxon's Master," and 20 more. 199pp. 5⅜ × 8½. 20767-6 Pa. $4.95

ETHICAL WRITINGS OF MAIMONIDES, Maimonides. Most significant ethical works of great medieval sage, newly translated for utmost precision, readability. Laws Concerning Character Traits, Eight Chapters, more. 192pp. 5⅜ × 8½.
24522-5 Pa. $5.95

THE EXPLORATION OF THE COLORADO RIVER AND ITS CANYONS, J. W. Powell. Full text of Powell's 1,000-mile expedition down the fabled Colorado in 1869. Superb account of terrain, geology, vegetation, Indians, famine, mutiny, treacherous rapids, mighty canyons, during exploration of last unknown part of continental U.S. 400pp. 5⅜ × 8½. 20094-9 Pa. $8.95

HISTORY OF PHILOSOPHY, Julián Marías. Clearest one-volume history on the market. Every major philosopher and dozens of others, to Existentialism and later. 505pp. 5⅜ × 8½. 21739-6 Pa. $9.95

ALL ABOUT LIGHTNING, Martin A. Uman. Highly readable nontechnical survey of nature and causes of lightning, thunderstorms, ball lightning, St. Elmo's Fire, much more. Illustrated. 192pp. 5⅜ × 8½. 25237-X Pa. $5.95

SAILING ALONE AROUND THE WORLD, Captain Joshua Slocum. First man to sail around the world, alone, in small boat. One of great feats of seamanship told in delightful manner. 67 illustrations. 294pp. 5⅜ × 8½. 20326-3 Pa. $4.95

LETTERS AND NOTES ON THE MANNERS, CUSTOMS AND CONDITIONS OF THE NORTH AMERICAN INDIANS, George Catlin. Classic account of life among Plains Indians: ceremonies, hunt, warfare, etc. 312 plates. 572pp. of text. 6⅛ × 9¼. 22118-0, 22119-9, Pa., Two-vol. set $17.90

THE SECRET LIFE OF SALVADOR DALÍ, Salvador Dalí. Outrageous but fascinating autobiography through Dalí's thirties with scores of drawings and sketches and 80 photographs. A must for lovers of 20th-century art. 432pp. 6½ × 9¼. (Available in U.S. only) 27454-3 Pa. $9.95

HOW TO WRITE, Gertrude Stein. Gertrude Stein claimed anyone could understand her unconventional writing—here are clues to help. Fascinating improvisations, language experiments, explanations illuminate Stein's craft and the art of writing. Total of 414pp. 4⅜ × 6⅜. 23144-5 Pa. $6.95

ADVENTURES AT SEA IN THE GREAT AGE OF SAIL: Five Firsthand Narratives, edited by Elliot Snow. Rare true accounts of exploration, whaling, shipwreck, fierce natives, trade, shipboard life, more. 33 illustrations. Introduction. 353pp. 5⅜ × 8½. 25177-2 Pa. $9.95

THE HERBAL OR GENERAL HISTORY OF PLANTS, John Gerard. Classic descriptions of about 2,850 plants—with over 2,700 illustrations—includes Latin and English names, physical descriptions, varieties, time and place of growth, more. 2,706 illustrations. xlv + 1,678pp. 8½ × 12¼. 23147-X Cloth. $89.95

DOROTHY AND THE WIZARD IN OZ, L. Frank Baum. Dorothy and the Wizard visit the center of the Earth, where people are vegetables, glass houses grow and Oz characters reappear. Classic sequel to *Wizard of Oz.* 256pp. 5⅜ × 8. 24714-7 Pa. $5.95

SONGS OF EXPERIENCE: Facsimile Reproduction with 26 Plates in Full Color, William Blake. This facsimile of Blake's original "Illuminated Book" reproduces 26 full-color plates from a rare 1826 edition. Includes "The Tyger," "London," "Holy Thursday," and other immortal poems. 26 color plates. Printed text of poems. 48pp. 5¼ × 7. 24636-1 Pa. $3.95

SONGS OF INNOCENCE, William Blake. The first and most popular of Blake's famous "Illuminated Books," in a facsimile edition reproducing all 31 brightly colored plates. Additional printed text of each poem. 64pp. 5¼ × 7. 22764-2 Pa. $3.95

PRECIOUS STONES, Max Bauer. Classic, thorough study of diamonds, rubies, emeralds, garnets, etc.: physical character, occurrence, properties, use, similar topics. 20 plates, 8 in color. 94 figures. 659pp. 6⅛ × 9¼. 21910-0, 21911-9 Pa., Two-vol. set $21.90

ENCYCLOPEDIA OF VICTORIAN NEEDLEWORK, S. F. A. Caulfeild and Blanche Saward. Full, precise descriptions of stitches, techniques for dozens of needlecrafts—most exhaustive reference of its kind. Over 800 figures. Total of 679pp. 8⅛ × 11. 22800-2, 22801-0 Pa., Two-vol. set $26.90

THE MARVELOUS LAND OF OZ, L. Frank Baum. Second Oz book, the Scarecrow and Tin Woodman are back with hero named Tip, Oz magic. 136 illustrations. 287pp. 5⅜ × 8½. 20692-0 Pa. $5.95

WILD FOWL DECOYS, Joel Barber. Basic book on the subject, by foremost authority and collector. Reveals history of decoy making and rigging, place in American culture, different kinds of decoys, how to make them, and how to use them. 140 plates. 156pp. 7⅞ × 10¾. 20011-6 Pa. $14.95

HISTORY OF LACE, Mrs. Bury Palliser. Definitive, profusely illustrated chronicle of lace from earliest times to late 19th century. Laces of Italy, Greece, England, France, Belgium, etc. Landmark of needlework scholarship. 266 illustrations. 672pp. 6⅛ × 9¼. 24742-2 Pa. $16.95

ILLUSTRATED GUIDE TO SHAKER FURNITURE, Robert Meader. All furniture and appurtenances, with much on unknown local styles. 235 photos. 146pp. 9 × 12. 22819-3 Pa. $9.95

WHALE SHIPS AND WHALING: A Pictorial Survey, George Francis Dow. Over 200 vintage engravings, drawings, photographs of barks, brigs, cutters, other vessels. Also harpoons, lances, whaling guns, many other artifacts. Comprehensive text by foremost authority. 207 black-and-white illustrations. 288pp. 6 × 9. 24808-9 Pa. $9.95

THE BERTRAMS, Anthony Trollope. Powerful portrayal of blind self-will and thwarted ambition includes one of Trollope's most heartrending love stories. 497pp. 5⅜ × 8½. 25119-5 Pa. $9.95

ADVENTURES WITH A HAND LENS, Richard Headstrom. Clearly written guide to observing and studying flowers and grasses, fish scales, moth and insect wings, egg cases, buds, feathers, seeds, leaf scars, moss, molds, ferns, common crystals, etc.—all with an ordinary, inexpensive magnifying glass. 209 exact line drawings aid in your discoveries. 220pp. 5⅜ × 8½. 23330-8 Pa. $5.95

RODIN ON ART AND ARTISTS, Auguste Rodin. Great sculptor's candid, wide-ranging comments on meaning of art; great artists; relation of sculpture to poetry, painting, music; philosophy of life, more. 76 superb black-and-white illustrations of Rodin's sculpture, drawings and prints. 119pp. 8⅜ × 11¼. 24487-3 Pa. $7.95

FIFTY CLASSIC FRENCH FILMS, 1912–1982: A Pictorial Record, Anthony Slide. Memorable stills from Grand Illusion, Beauty and the Beast, Hiroshima, Mon Amour, many more. Credits, plot synopses, reviews, etc. 160pp. 8¼ × 11. 25256-6 Pa. $11.95

THE PRINCIPLES OF PSYCHOLOGY, William James. Famous long course complete, unabridged. Stream of thought, time perception, memory, experimental methods; great work decades ahead of its time. 94 figures. 1,391pp. 5⅜ × 8½. 20381-6, 20382-4 Pa., Two-vol. set $25.90

BODIES IN A BOOKSHOP, R. T. Campbell. Challenging mystery of blackmail and murder with ingenious plot and superbly drawn characters. In the best tradition of British suspense fiction. 192pp. 5⅜ × 8½. 24720-1 Pa. $5.95

CALLAS: Portrait of a Prima Donna, George Jellinek. Renowned commentator on the musical scene chronicles incredible career and life of the most controversial, fascinating, influential operatic personality of our time. 64 black-and-white photographs. 416pp. 5⅜ × 8¼. 25047-4 Pa. $8.95

GEOMETRY, RELATIVITY AND THE FOURTH DIMENSION, Rudolph Rucker. Exposition of fourth dimension, concepts of relativity as Flatland characters continue adventures. Popular, easily followed yet accurate, profound. 141 illustrations. 133pp. 5⅜ × 8½. 23400-2 Pa. $4.95

HOUSEHOLD STORIES BY THE BROTHERS GRIMM, with pictures by Walter Crane. 53 classic stories—Rumpelstiltskin, Rapunzel, Hansel and Gretel, the Fisherman and his Wife, Snow White, Tom Thumb, Sleeping Beauty, Cinderella, and so much more—lavishly illustrated with original 19th-century drawings. 114 illustrations. x + 269pp. 5⅜ × 8½. 21080-4 Pa. $4.95

CATALOG OF DOVER BOOKS

DEGAS: An Intimate Portrait, Ambroise Vollard. Charming, anecdotal memoir by
famous art dealer of one of the greatest 19th-century French painters. 14 black-and-
white illustrations. Introduction by Harold L. Van Doren. 96pp. 5⅜ × 8½.
25131-4 Pa. $4.95

PERSONAL NARRATIVE OF A PILGRIMAGE TO AL–MADINAH AND
MECCAH, Richard F. Burton. Great travel classic by remarkably colorful
personality. Burton, disguised as a Moroccan, visited sacred shrines of Islam,
narrowly escaping death. 47 illustrations. 959pp. 5⅜ × 8½.
21217-3, 21218-1 Pa., Two-vol. set $19.90

PHRASE AND WORD ORIGINS, A. H. Holt. Entertaining, reliable, modern
study of more than 1,200 colorful words, phrases, origins and histories. Much
unexpected information. 254pp. 5⅜ × 8½. 20758-7 Pa. $5.95

THE RED THUMB MARK, R. Austin Freeman. In this first Dr. Thorndyke case,
the great scientific detective draws fascinating conclusions from the nature of a
single fingerprint. Exciting story, authentic science. 320pp. 5⅜ × 8½. (Available in
U.S. only) 25210-8 Pa. $6.95

AN EGYPTIAN HIEROGLYPHIC DICTIONARY, E. A. Wallis Budge. Monu-
mental work containing about 25,000 words or terms that occur in texts ranging
from 3000 B.C. to 600 A.D. Each entry consists of a transliteration of the word, the
word in hieroglyphs, and the meaning in English. 1,314pp. 6⅞ × 10.
23615-3, 23616-1 Pa., Two-vol. set $35.90

THE COMPLEAT STRATEGYST: Being a Primer on the Theory of Games of
Strategy, J. D. Williams. Highly entertaining classic describes, with many
illustrated examples, how to select best strategies in conflict situations. Prefaces.
Appendices. xvi + 268pp. 5⅜ × 8½. 25101-2 Pa. $7.95

THE ROAD TO OZ, L. Frank Baum. Dorothy meets the Shaggy Man, little
Button-Bright and the Rainbow's beautiful daughter in this delightful trip to the
magical Land of Oz. 272pp. 5⅜ × 8. 25208-6 Pa. $5.95

POINT AND LINE TO PLANE, Wassily Kandinsky. Seminal exposition of role of
point, line, other elements in nonobjective painting. Essential to understanding
20th-century art. 127 illustrations. 192pp. 6½ × 9¼. 23808-3 Pa. $5.95

LADY ANNA, Anthony Trollope. Moving chronicle of Countess Lovel's bitter
struggle to win for herself and daughter Anna their rightful rank and fortune—
perhaps at cost of sanity itself. 384pp. 5⅜ × 8½. 24669-8 Pa. $8.95

EGYPTIAN MAGIC, E. A. Wallis Budge. Sums up all that is known about magic
in Ancient Egypt: the role of magic in controlling the gods, powerful amulets that
warded off evil spirits, scarabs of immortality, use of wax images, formulas and
spells, the secret name, much more. 253pp. 5⅜ × 8½. 22681-6 Pa. $4.95

THE DANCE OF SIVA, Ananda Coomaraswamy. Preeminent authority unfolds
the vast metaphysic of India: the revelation of her art, conception of the universe,
social organization, etc. 27 reproductions of art masterpieces. 192pp. 5⅜ × 8½.
24817-8 Pa. $6.95

CATALOG OF DOVER BOOKS

THE ART NOUVEAU STYLE BOOK OF ALPHONSE MUCHA: All 72 Plates from "Documents Decoratifs" in Original Color, Alphonse Mucha. Rare copyright-free design portfolio by high priest of Art Nouveau. Jewelry, wallpaper, stained glass, furniture, figure studies, plant and animal motifs, etc. Only complete one-volume edition. 80pp. 9⅜ × 12¼.   24044-4 Pa. $10.95

ANIMALS: 1,419 Copyright-Free Illustrations of Mammals, Birds, Fish, Insects, Etc., edited by Jim Harter. Clear wood engravings present, in extremely lifelike poses, over 1,000 species of animals. One of the most extensive pictorial sourcebooks of its kind. Captions. Index. 284pp. 9 × 12.   23766-4 Pa. $10.95

OBELISTS FLY HIGH, C. Daly King. Masterpiece of American detective fiction, long out of print, involves murder on a 1935 transcontinental flight—"a very thrilling story"—NY Times. Unabridged and unaltered republication of the edition published by William Collins Sons & Co. Ltd., London, 1935. 288pp. 5⅜ × 8½.
(Available in U.S. only)   25036-9 Pa. $5.95

VICTORIAN AND EDWARDIAN FASHION: A Photographic Survey, Alison Gernsheim. First fashion history completely illustrated by contemporary photographs. Full text plus 235 photos, 1840–1914, in which many celebrities appear. 240pp. 6½ × 9¼.   24205-6 Pa. $8.95

THE ART OF THE FRENCH ILLUSTRATED BOOK, 1700–1914, Gordon N. Ray. Over 630 superb book illustrations by Fragonard, Delacroix, Daumier, Doré, Grandville, Manet, Mucha, Steinlen, Toulouse-Lautrec and many others. Preface. Introduction. 633 halftones. Indices of artists, authors & titles, binders and provenances. Appendices. Bibliography. 608pp. 8⅜ × 11¼.   25086-5 Pa. $24.95

THE WONDERFUL WIZARD OF OZ, L. Frank Baum. Facsimile in full color of America's finest children's classic. 143 illustrations by W. W. Denslow. 267pp. 5⅜ × 8½.   20691-2 Pa. $7.95

FOLLOWING THE EQUATOR: A Journey Around the World, Mark Twain. Great writer's 1897 account of circumnavigating the globe by steamship. Ironic humor, keen observations, vivid and fascinating descriptions of exotic places. 197 illustrations. 720pp. 5⅜ × 8½.   26113-1 Pa. $15.95

THE FRIENDLY STARS, Martha Evans Martin & Donald Howard Menzel. Classic text marshalls the stars together in an engaging, nontechnical survey, presenting them as sources of beauty in night sky. 23 illustrations. Foreword. 2 star charts. Index. 147pp. 5⅜ × 8½.   21099-5 Pa. $3.95

FADS AND FALLACIES IN THE NAME OF SCIENCE, Martin Gardner. Fair, witty appraisal of cranks, quacks, and quackeries of science and pseudoscience: hollow earth, Velikovsky, orgone energy, Dianetics, flying saucers, Bridey Murphy, food and medical fads, etc. Revised, expanded In the Name of Science. "A very able and even-tempered presentation."—The New Yorker. 363pp. 5⅜ × 8.
                                                                  20394-8 Pa. $6.95

ANCIENT EGYPT: Its Culture and History, J. E. Manchip White. From predynastics through Ptolemies: society, history, political structure, religion, daily life, literature, cultural heritage. 48 plates. 217pp. 5⅜ × 8½.   22548-8 Pa. $5.95

CATALOG OF DOVER BOOKS

AMERICAN CLIPPER SHIPS: 1833–1858, Octavius T. Howe & Frederick C. Matthews. Fully-illustrated, encyclopedic review of 352 clipper ships from the period of America's greatest maritime supremacy. Introduction. 109 halftones. 5 black-and-white line illustrations. Index. Total of 928pp. 5⅜ × 8½.
25115-2, 25116-0 Pa., Two-vol. set $21.90

TOWARDS A NEW ARCHITECTURE, Le Corbusier. Pioneering manifesto by great architect, near legendary founder of "International School." Technical and aesthetic theories, views on industry, economics, relation of form to function, "mass-production spirit," much more. Profusely illustrated. Unabridged translation of 13th French edition. Introduction by Frederick Etchells. 320pp. 6⅛ × 9¼.
(Available in U.S. only)   25023-7 Pa. $8.95

THE BOOK OF KELLS, edited by Blanche Cirker. Inexpensive collection of 32 full-color, full-page plates from the greatest illuminated manuscript of the Middle Ages, painstakingly reproduced from rare facsimile edition. Publisher's Note. Captions. 32pp. 9⅜ × 12¼. (Available in U.S. only)   24345-1 Pa. $5.95

BEST SCIENCE FICTION STORIES OF H. G. WELLS, H. G. Wells. Full novel *The Invisible Man*, plus 17 short stories: "The Crystal Egg," "Aepyornis Island," "The Strange Orchid," etc. 303pp. 5⅜ × 8½. (Available in U.S. only)
21531-8 Pa. $6.95

AMERICAN SAILING SHIPS: Their Plans and History, Charles G. Davis. Photos, construction details of schooners, frigates, clippers, other sailcraft of 18th to early 20th centuries—plus entertaining discourse on design, rigging, nautical lore, much more. 137 black-and-white illustrations. 240pp. 6⅛ × 9¼.
24658-2 Pa. $6.95

ENTERTAINING MATHEMATICAL PUZZLES, Martin Gardner. Selection of author's favorite conundrums involving arithmetic, money, speed, etc., with lively commentary. Complete solutions. 112pp. 5⅜ × 8½.   25211-6 Pa. $3.95

THE WILL TO BELIEVE, HUMAN IMMORTALITY, William James. Two books bound together. Effect of irrational on logical, and arguments for human immortality. 402pp. 5⅜ × 8½.   20291-7 Pa. $8.95

THE HAUNTED MONASTERY and THE CHINESE MAZE MURDERS, Robert Van Gulik. 2 full novels by Van Gulik continue adventures of Judge Dee and his companions. An evil Taoist monastery, seemingly supernatural events; overgrown topiary maze that hides strange crimes. Set in 7th-century China. 27 illustrations. 328pp. 5⅜ × 8½.   23502-5 Pa. $6.95

CELEBRATED CASES OF JUDGE DEE (DEE GOONG AN), translated by Robert Van Gulik. Authentic 18th-century Chinese detective novel; Dee and associates solve three interlocked cases. Led to Van Gulik's own stories with same characters. Extensive introduction. 9 illustrations. 237pp. 5⅜ × 8½.
23337-5 Pa. $5.95

Prices subject to change without notice.

Available at your book dealer or write for free catalog to Dept. GI, Dover Publications, Inc., 31 East 2nd St., Mineola, N.Y. 11501. Dover publishes more than 400 books each year on science, elementary and advanced mathematics, biology, music, art, literary history, social sciences and other areas.